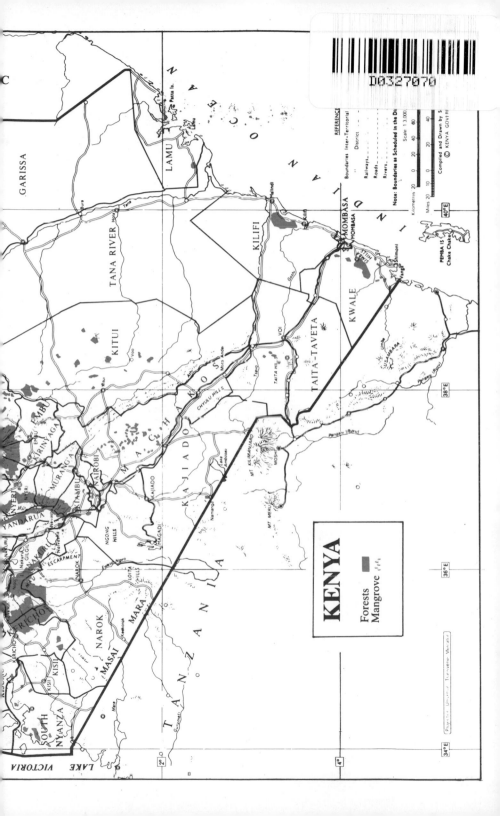

KENYA

Forests
Mangrove

REFERENCE

Boundaries Inter-Territorial _____
District _____
Railways _____
Roads _____
Rivers _____

Note: Boundaries as Scheduled in the Di...

Scale 1:3,000,...

Kilometres 20 0 20 40 60
Miles 20 10 0 20 40

Compiled and Drawn by S...
© KENYA GOVT...

Projection Universal Transverse Mercator

LAKE VICTORIA

GARISSA

LAMU

TANA RIVER

KILIFI

KITUI

KWALE

TAITA-TAVETA

MACHAKOS

KAJIADO

EMBU

KIRINYAGA

MURANGA

NYANDARUA

NAKURU

NAROK

MASAI MARA

KISII

SOUTH NYANZA

KERICHO

T A N Z A N I A

I N D I A N   O C E A N

MOMBASA

MT. KILIMANJARO

MT. MERU

MOSHI

PEMBA IS
Chake Chake

40°E

38°E

36°E

34°E

2°

4°

THE
WILD FLOWERS
OF KENYA

THE
WILD FLOWERS
OF KENYA

Michael Blundell

with additional photographs by
Tim Campbell, Peter Davey & Nigel Pavitt

COLLINS
St James's Place, London

William Collins Sons & Co Ltd
London · Glasgow · Sydney · Auckland
Toronto · Johannesburg

This book is dedicated to

ERNEST KLEINWORT

*who did so much for, and contributed
so much to, the conservation and
preservation of wildlife throughout the world.*

First published 1982
(Sir Michael Blundell, K.B.E., 1982
ISBN 0 00 219317 5
Filmset by Servis Filmsetting Ltd, Manchester
Colour reproduction by Adroit Photo Litho Ltd, Birmingham
Printed and bound by
William Collins Sons and Co Ltd, Glasgow

Preface

I have long felt the need for a book which would give the resident of, or traveller in Kenya an introduction to the beautiful wild flowers of the country; a book which would not demand a training in botany but be as approachable for the general reader as for the expert botanist. I have therefore set out to present the beauty of Kenya's wild flowers primarily through colour photographs, which will provide an invaluable guide to recognition of the various species. A description of each plant, presented in reasonably simple language and concentrating on the type of growth and leaf form of the individual species, provides a text to complement the illustrations. I have included not only descriptions of every plant portrayed but also of many allied species which may be found growing in similar conditions or at lower and higher altitudes in the hope that this will help the reader to broaden his knowledge of the flowers and encourage a greater interest in this wonderful heritage.

It is obvious that a single volume of this size cannot include every one of the thousands of plants which occur in Kenya; indeed most of the grasses and sedges and many of the trees and bushes would not be considered flowers by many people. I have therefore selected for illustration those that will most commonly be seen, with some description of their most noticeable relatives. Also included are some of the rarer and more unusual species as these are exciting to find and interesting to see.

The illustrations have been arranged according to their colour in a sequence from white to yellow and through orange to red, magenta purple and blue. The text describing species is presented in taxonomic order, family by family. Species not illustrated are also listed in colour sequence.

To aid identification a simple key based upon conspicuous features is included which may be used in conjunction with the contents list to guide readers to broad groups of families. An index of flowers by colour and family includes all species in the book. The text avoids the unnecessary use of complex scientific terms unknown to the general reader but some descriptions are greatly simplified by using correct botanical nomenclature and a comprehensive glossary is included to explain all technical terms. Illustrations of the shapes and patterns of leaves, the types of inflorescence and the parts of a flower will also help the reader to understand them.

Acknowledgements

In producing this book I owe a great debt of gratitude to many kind friends and helpers. In particular I should like to thank the following:

Guinness (E.A.) Ltd, Kenya Breweries Ltd and the Kenya Horticultural Society for their generous financial support, without which the book might not have been published

Peter Davey, Nigel Pavitt and Tim Campbell, the photographers, who have so kindly provided the excellent photographs and who have so willingly gone into all areas, including the 'far places' to provide material both interesting and, at times, unusual. Without their work the book would not have come to life.

Miss C.H.S. Kabuye, the Botanist in-charge and all the staff at the Herbarium in Nairobi, which is attached to the Kenya National Museum, for their great help and assistance in classifying and naming the plants shown in the photographs. Mr J.B. Gillett I must especially mention. He has helped me with the greatest enthusiasm in identification and in particular in research into the size of flowers, habitat and altitude ranges. Without his assistance and enthusiasm and the help of Miss Kabuye and the staff of the Herbarium the book would have been much reduced in its botanical descriptions. Their criticisms and scientific knowledge have been invaluable.

Mrs Susan Goodwin, who has so cheerfully and accurately carried out all the typing and secretarial work for me in a field where much of the nomenclature was unfamiliar to her, and to my wife who has tolerated my withdrawal into long spells of isolation while writing and checking the text.

The Department of Survey, in Kenya, who so kindly and with so much friendliness produced the material for the maps, which I hope will help readers in understanding the distribution of the plants and the ecological zones in which they grow.

The author, Mr A.D.Q. Agnew, and publishers, the Oxford University Press, for permission to use the invaluable information contained in *Upland Wild Flowers of Kenya*.

Mr Robert MacDonald and his staff at Collins, who gave much help and advice in the preparation of the text and photographs.

Contents

CONTENTS

Key to Groups of Families

This key should be used in conjunction with the contents list, the numbers given below referring to the numbering of the families therein.

Leaves usually not parallel-sided, veins forming a network, usually not parallel. Parts of the flower usually in fives or fours, very rarely in threes. Often trees, shrubs or shrublets. Seed leaves two = DICOTYLEDONS   Families 1–60

　　Petals free from one another or absent (or if petals united then stamens twice as many as petals and carpels free or single, or stamens numerous = DICOTYLEDONS: ARCHICHLAMYDEAE (and one GYMNOSPERM)   Families 1–40

　　Petals united, sometimes only at the base; carpels united, at least through the styles. Stamens never more than twice as many as the corolla lobes = DICOTYLEDONS: GAMOPETALAE   Families 41–60

　　　　Flowers regular, stamens as many as the corolla lobes or, rarely, twice as many: Families 41–53

　　　　Flowers zygomorphic, stamens (except in *Verbascum*) fewer than the corolla lobes: Families 54–60

Leaves usually narrow and more or less parallelsided, with parallel veins. Parts of the flower usually in threes or sixes. Rarely trees or shrubs and if so of an unusual type (e.g. Palms). Seed leaf single = MONOCOTYLEDONS   Families 61–67

Introduction

No one yet knows exactly how many species of flowering plant occur in Kenya. There are certainly some growing which have not yet been named scientifically and there are others which grow in adjacent countries which have not yet been recorded in Kenya. There are cases in which a single species has been given more than one scientific name so that the number of species appears to be higher than it really is and there is dispute over whether certain forms have specific status. However, when the botanists who are now working to produce *The Flora of Tropical East Africa* eventually complete their work – which may well not be before the end of this century – we shall find that between 8,000 and 9,000 species of flowering plant occur in Kenya.

The flora of Kenya is so interesting because of the wide range of ecological and climatic conditions which are encountered in the country. The two major factors governing the distribution and growth of our plants are rainfall and altitude. Recognition of plants can often be assisted by a knowledge of the zones in which they are likely to be found. These may be broadly divided into:

Alpine Zone, above 3,650m (12,000ft).

Highlands, including moorlands, higher rainfall forest and upland grassy plains; altitude *c.* 1,800–3,650m (6,000–12,000ft), rainfall above *c.* 1,000mm (40in).

Moister Bushed Woodland and Grassland, medium to higher rainfall areas; altitude *c.* 1,100–2,000m (3,600–6,500ft), rainfall 625–1,000mm (25–40in).

Drier Bushed Woodland and Grassland, medium dry to medium rainfall areas; altitude *c.* 760–1,800m (2,500–6,000ft), rainfall 400–625mm (16–25in).

Dry Bushland, low rainfall areas; altitude generally below 1,060m (*c.* 3,500ft), rainfall 250–400mm (10–16in).

Arid bushland or Dwarf Shrub Grassland, rainfall below 250mm (10in), altitude generally below 760m (2,500ft).

It should be noted that the coastal zone, where the moisture index is rarely less than 10 and the conditions are moist, warm, and tropical with a rainfall of 1,000mm (40in) upwards, is an area extending inland all along the coast of Kenya for an approximate distance of 16–24km (10–15 miles). After this the Drier Bushed Woodland and Grassland and Dry Bushland zones are predominant.

True deserts – areas devoid of plants, except in specially favoured spots –

11

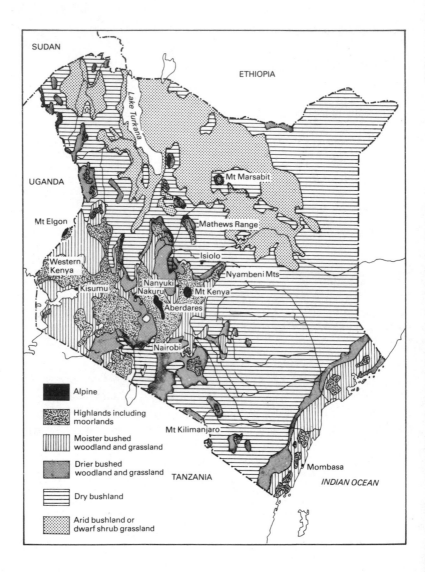

SUDAN

ETHIOPIA

UGANDA

Lake Turkana

Mt Marsabit

Mt Elgon

Mathews Range

Western Kenya

Isiolo

Nyambeni Mts

Kisumu

Nanyuki
Nakuru

Mt Kenya

Aberdares

Nairobi

Alpine

Highlands including
moorlands

Moister bushed
woodland and grassland

Drier bushed
woodland and grassland

Mt Kilimanjaro

Dry bushland

Mombasa

Arid bushland or
dwarf shrub grassland

TANZANIA

INDIAN OCEAN

do not exist in Kenya, although there are semi-deserts in the north where only scattered herbs and shrubs are found which, although leaving much of the surface of the ground bare, maintain a network of roots beneath. Dry bushland, where there is usually a fair amount of vegetation, especially after the infrequent rains, is sometimes wrongly called desert because it can support only a very sparse human population.

Kenya does not have true rain forest either but the forest can be divided into areas of higher rainfall, (more than 1,000mm (40in) per annum, where considerable mist and cloud persist, and areas which, although evergreen, have rainfall around 750mm (30in), and are known as dry forests. Examples of the former are Mt Elgon, the Aberdares, Mt Kenya and the Mau, and of the latter Langata (Nairobi National Park), the Chyulu Hills and parts of the Nyeri District below 2,000m (6,500ft). It should always be remembered that as the altitude increases so the effect of rainfall is also proportionately enhanced.

Moving westwards in Kenya the mean night temperature tends to rise as the mellowing influence of the great body of water contained in Lake Victoria begins to affect the climate. Thus it may well happen that medium-altitude plants in eastern Kenya will be found at slightly higher altitudes in the west. The altitude ranges given in this book are based on collection notes attached to specimens in the East African Herbarium, at Kew and elsewhere as well as from personal observation. Further studies and collecting will improve them but since in many cases only a few altitudes have been recorded for a species and the person recording it usually knew it only approximately, it is impossible to define them clearly. The normal range may also be altered by so many circumstances. For instance, where a cool stream flows at the bottom of a narrow gorge with limited sunshine the plants from higher altitudes may well spread down the stream to lower levels; similarly in the upper regions, on warm hillsides facing the full effect of the morning or afternoon sun, the opposite may occur, a plant becoming established some quite considerable height above its recorded altitude. For these reasons the altitudes given in the text are intended as a guide only, conversions from metric to imperial measure are not exact but to approximate, easily comprehensible ranges.

Many of the brightly-coloured orange and orange-red flowers in Kenya, such as the Aloes, Leonotis and most of the Loranthaceae are particularly attractive to birds such as the Sunbirds (Nectarinea) which are able to distinguish these colours. Many Kenyan plants also have an unusually generous supply of nectar compared with those of more temperate areas such as Europe and North America and thus can support an above average population of bees.

Enthusiastic plant and flower lovers have sometimes been guilty of indiscriminate and unwise uprooting and collecting which has unwittingly done considerable damage to species such as some of the Orchids, Caralluma, *Adenium obesum* (Desert Rose), Cyrtanthus and the Cycads. Where a house is being built, a road widened or a forest cut down an attempt at moving a plant may save it, but otherwise they are best left in the wild where they are. Many of the more rare and beautiful plants will not easily tolerate a change in environment or soil conditions. They die. Far better to leave them where they have chosen to develop on their own so that everyone visiting the area can enjoy them.

THE NAMING OF PLANTS

To avoid the confusion of differing local common names and linguistic variations every species of plant is known internationally by a scientific name consisting of two latin words, often called the 'Binomial System'. The first word, which is given a capital letter, identifies the genus to which the plant belongs and the latin form may be either masculine, feminine or neuter. The second word indicates the species to which the plant belongs, which is not written with a capital. It is usually a latin adjective the ending of which must agree with the gender of the latin generic name. Thus *Ranunculus multifidus* has the male ending *-us*, because *Ranunculus* is masculine; *Anemone brachiata* has the female ending *-a*, because *Anemone* is feminine and *Sedum ruwenzoriense* has the neuter ending *-e*, because *Sedum* is neuter. The second word may be the latinized form of the name of the botanist who first described and located the plant, as in the case of *fischeri*, *hildebrandtii* or *battiscombei*, which are the latin possessive forms, or a specific description of the flower or the growth of the plant, for example *multiflorus* (many-flowered), *repens* (creeping) and *foetidum* (evil-smelling), or an indication of its locality as with *Lobelia keniensis* (Kenyan), and *Notonia abyssinica* (of Abyssinia). Occasionally a word of greek origin creeps into the specific name as in *Acacia xanthophloea*, from the Greek for 'yellow bark or skin'.

While the species indicates a different form within a genus there may also be a third name to indicate a subdivision within a species known as a subspecies and where differences are not such that a separate species or subspecies is warranted but there is a distinct variation in a plant it may also sometimes be described as a variety.

Groups of related genera are called Families which are usually named from the type genus with its end changed to aceae. Thus Ranunculaceae is short for *Plantae Ranunculaceae*, latin for 'plants like *Ranunculus*'. However, a few well-known family names were formed in other ways. Thus Umbelliferae means plants carrying umbels and Labiatae plants with lips, while Palmae and Gramineae are the latin names for Palms and Grasses. Many modern botanists consider that all the family names should follow one procedure: alternative names have therefore been recognised which are based upon a single system – Apiaceae, Lamiaceae, Arecaceae and Poaceae for the four families just mentioned.

Groups of related families are called Orders and their names usually end in -ales. Thus the order Cycadales embraces the related families of Cycadaceae, Zamiaceae and Stangeriaceae. Large families may be subdivided into tribes,

14

which are groups of genera which resemble each other more than they resemble the rest of the family. The names of tribes end in -eae and thus we have the Phaseoleae, a tribe within the Papilionaceae.

IDENTIFYING PLANTS

The illustrations and the descriptions in this book will help you to identify the flowers found in Kenya. The photographs have been arranged by colour which is one immediate approach which you can use, although there are plants which can appear in several colour forms and more careful study will frequently be required. The colour index will guide you to both listed and unlisted species which are arranged in order of family under each colour heading. The descriptions in the text will guide you as to both the districts and the altitudes in which particular species are likely to be found, their size and overall appearance, their leaf and flower structure and other pertinent features by which they may be recognised. Try to recognise the features of the various families. The key following the contents list and linked with it will guide you to particular family groups. Use this in conjunction with the colour index. Allow for habitat requirements which will further restrict the possibilities. Carefully study the leaf shape and arrangement and the formation and placing of the flowers. Positive identification will not always be possible to specific level but in attempting it you will gain a deeper understanding of Kenya's plants.

For a detailed investigation to determine the family to which a plant belongs a hand lens (a magnification × 10 is most suitable) and a mounted needle for opening up flowers will be found most useful. The keys to families in *Upland Kenya Wild Flowers* and *Some Common Flowering Plants of Uganda* may then be consulted. The first is now difficult to obtain but the latter is readily available in Nairobi.

Readers who wish to pursue their study in more detail than is attempted in this book should consult these two books and others listed under Further Reading.

If other methods of naming plants fail, the Botanist in Charge, East African Herbarium, Box 45166, Nairobi (situated behind the National Museum) is prepared to name properly dried specimens if details of place of collection etc are supplied and if the Herbarium is allowed to retain the specimens. If a plant is found in an area or at an altitude from which it has not previously been recorded, or with a previously unrecorded African name or use, an annotated specimen which serves as a permanent record of this information is always especially welcome at the Herbarium.

PARTS OF A FLOWER

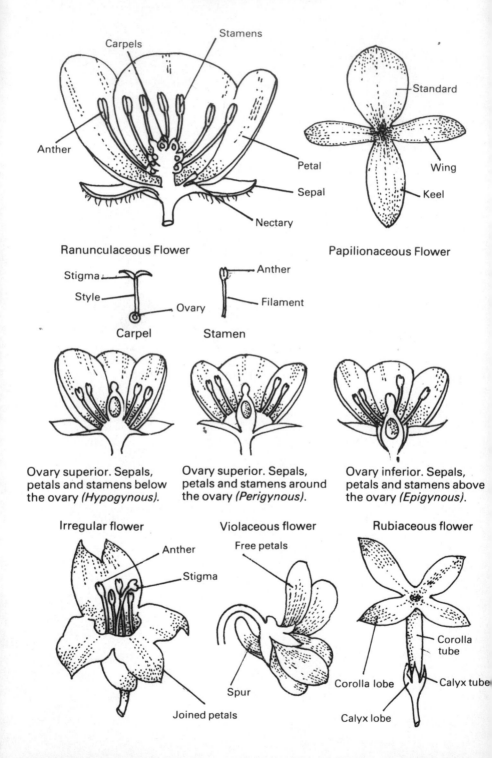

Carpels

Stamens

Anther

Petal

Sepal

Nectary

Ranunculaceous Flower

Standard

Wing

Keel

Papilionaceous Flower

Stigma

Style

Ovary

Carpel

Anther

Filament

Stamen

Ovary superior. Sepals, petals and stamens below the ovary *(Hypogynous).*

Ovary superior. Sepals, petals and stamens around the ovary *(Perigynous).*

Ovary inferior. Sepals, petals and stamens above the ovary *(Epigynous).*

Irregular flower

Anther

Stigma

Joined petals

Violaceous flower

Free petals

Spur

Rubiaceous flower

Corolla tube

Corolla lobe

Calyx tube

Calyx lobe

FORMS OF INFLORESCENCE

Spike

Raceme   Corymb

Panicle

Dichasial cyme

Scorpiod cyme

Umbel

Compound umbel

Umbel on a scape

Scape

Bracteoles

Bracts

Bracteate umbel

Composite head *(Capitulum)*
Compositae

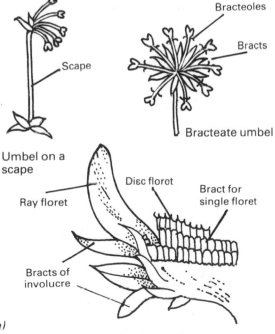

Ray floret

Disc floret

Bract for single floret

Bracts of involucre

Capitulum in section

LEAF FORMS AND ARRANGEMENTS

Simple alternate leaves

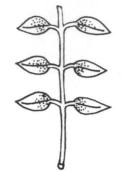

Simple opposite leaves

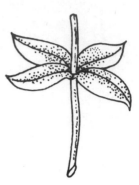

Whorled leaves

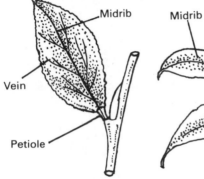

Midrib

Vein

Petiole

Simple alternate leaf

Midrib　　　Axil

Simple opposite leaf

Interpetiole stipule

Leaf showing
interpetiole stipule

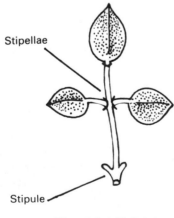

Stipellae

Stipule

Pinnately trifoliolate

Palmately trifoliolate

LEAF FORMS AND COMPOUND LEAVES

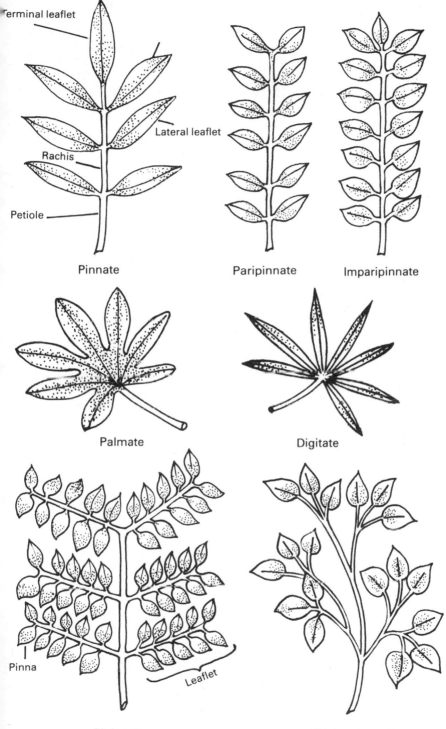

Terminal leaflet

Lateral leaflet

Rachis

Petiole

Pinnate

Paripinnate

Imparipinnate

Palmate

Digitate

Pinna

Leaflet

Dipinnate

Tripinnate

LEAF SHAPES

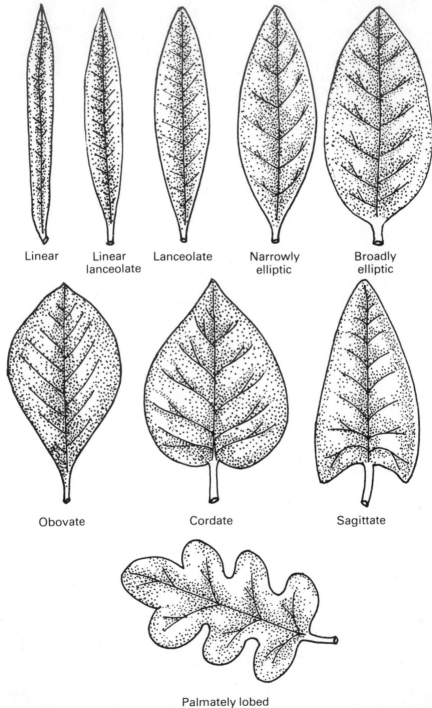

Linear

Linear lanceolate

Lanceolate

Narrowly elliptic

Broadly elliptic

Obovate

Cordate

Sagittate

Palmately lobed

LEAF SHAPES

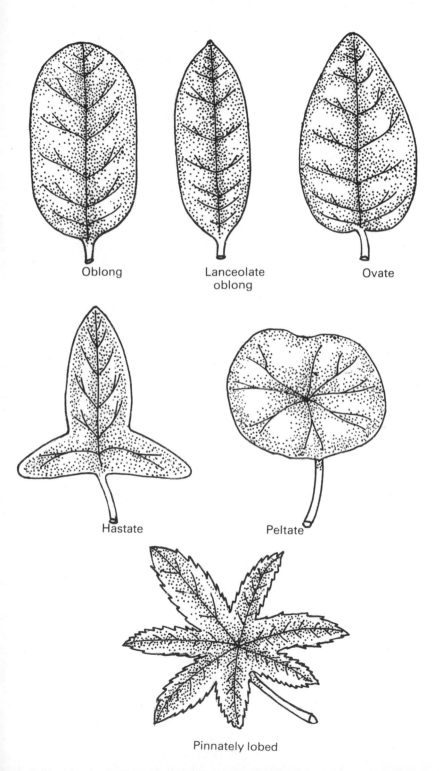

Oblong

Lanceolate oblong

Ovate

Hastate

Peltate

Pinnately lobed

LEAF TIPS

Acuminate Acute Obtuse Truncate Retuse

LEAF BASES

Cordate Sagittate Hastate

LEAF MARGINS

Entire Undulate Crenate Serrate Dentate

LEAF TIPS

Emarginate   Apiculate   Mucronate   Caudate (or Cuspidate)

LEAF BASES

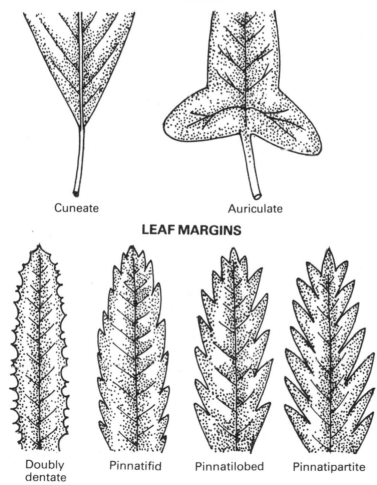

Cuneate   Auriculate

LEAF MARGINS

Doubly dentate   Pinnatifid   Pinnatilobed   Pinnatipartite

Notes on the Text

1   Where the name of a species has one or more other names in brackets after it, it signifies that the name has recently been changed by botanists, the old name being recorded for reference purposes in brackets. Examples are: *Cordia africana (C. holstii, C. abyssinica)*, and *Scadoxus multiflorus (Haemanthus multiflorus)*.

2   Where a plant has not as yet been given a scientific name or when a scientific name has not as yet been definitely established, I have adopted from the Editor of the *Flora of Tropical East Africa*, the practice of designating it as a Species 'A' or Species 'B' etc., e.g. *Bidens species A*.

It must be realised that when new plants are discovered in a country like Kenya, botanists hesitate to name them specifically until they have researched the botanical records of other countries, a process which may take time, in order to satisfy themselves that the plant has not already been named.

3   Where a plant is recorded from the photograph as a species only, e.g. *Dyschoriste* sp., *Vernonia* sp., it means that, herbarium material being unavailable, it was impossible to make an exact identification from the photograph only. I have included them in these instances, however, as the general picture of the flower will help the reader to a generic if not specific identification.

4   It must be understood that altitude figures both in metres and feet are meant to be an indication only of the altitude range. Neither they nor the conversions from metres to feet can possibly be precise. The reasons for this are fully explained in the introduction. Metric figures for sizes of flowers and inflorescences may be taken as accurate, conversions are to the nearest convenient fraction. For readers requiring precise conversions and for use with other texts giving only one form of measurement conversion tables are provided at the end of the text.

5   Where a plant is not tolerant of salt carried in the air from the sea, the altitude is shown as 1m (3ft) upwards.

6   Where an asterisk * appears against the name of the plant, it indicates that there may be a slight doubt on identification as field material was not available and identification has been made from the photograph alone.

1. CYCADACEAE

The Cycadaceae are a very ancient plant family. Examples have been found in fossil forms millions of years old. They and the Ginkgo are the only seed plants in which the male gametes are mobile, like those of ferns, mosses and algae. There are ten genera among the cycads consisting of more than 100 species which are scattered about the tropics and subtropics. They all have massive unbranched stems, pinnate leaves, naked ovules (usually in the form of cones) and very large seeds. There are only two genera in Kenya: *Encephalartos* with three or four species and *Cycas* with one species found at the coast.

Encephalartos tegulaneus   Plate 15 (94)
A cycad with a cylindrical stem growing up to 7.6m (25ft) and up to 30cm (1ft) in diameter which is covered with leaf scars and abscissed leaves and scale leaves in alternating zones. Scale leaves are lanceolate-acuminate to linear 15cm (6in) long. Other leaves are linear-oblanceolate, up to 1.5m (5ft) long and 30cm (1ft) wide. The male cone is nearly cylindrical, tapering abruptly at the apex and gradually at the base, 35cm (14in) long and 10cm (4in) wide. The scales on the cone overlap like roof tiles. The female cone is slightly smaller and wider – up to 15cm (6in). This cycad is found in dry or medium dry areas at 400–2,100m (1,200–7,000ft) on rocky hills or in cedar, phoenix or euphorbia forest near springs, in the Mathews Range and neighbouring mountains.

E. hildebrandtii is not uncommon in drier forest belts and in bush in coastal districts. The Brazil-nut-like kernel may be boiled, dried and ground for use as flour and the pith of the stem also provides food in time of famine. Altitude range 1–300m (3–1,000ft). Male cone size: 20–50cm (c. 8–20in) long, 5–9cm (2–3½in) diameter. Female cone: 28–60cm (c. 11–24in) long, 15–25cm (c. 6–10in) diameter.

2. RANUNCULACEAE
The Buttercup Family

A medium-sized mainly temperate family of herbs or, rarely, climbers; often more or less poisonous. Leaves are usually alternate, with sheathing bases, usually divided. Sepals and petals (if present) are free, stamens numerous, spirally arranged, and carpels from one to many. In Kenya 17 species of Ranunculaceae occur, representing six genera, one of them the Delphinium with its well-known, handsome, blue or white, spurred flowers.

Clematis brachiata *(C. hirsuta)*   **Plate 7** (47)
The African equivalent of the Old Man's Beard of European hedgerows, this
is a climbing plant of some magnificence. Each leaf has five to seven rounded
to ovate leaflets and panicles of creamy white flowers grow on long stems. It
can often be seen crowning the tops of small trees and large shrubs with a
mass of flowers, followed by the fluffy seed heads of the type which gave Old
Man's Beard its name. It is widespread from 1,000–2,100m (3,280–7,000ft) in
forest glades and edges and wooded grassland in areas of medium rainfall,
though it can also be seen in lava at Kibwezi. Flower: 22–50mm ($\frac{7}{8}$–2in)
across.

C. sinensis also grows in similar conditions at forest edges and roadsides in
upland rain forest. It is a shrubby climber, though it can be a strong liane. The
dark, shiny green leaves have up to five leaflets and are larger and more
oblong-elliptic than *C. hirsuta*. They immediately distinguish it from that
climber. Altitude range 1,600–3,250m (5,250–10,650ft). Flower: 20–36mm
($\frac{7}{8}$–1$\frac{3}{8}$in) fully open. Sepals: 7–16mm ($\frac{1}{4}$–$\frac{5}{8}$in) long.

Delphinium macrocentron   **Plate 48** (310)
A delightful member of the genus *Delphinium* which grows up to 2m (6$\frac{1}{2}$ft)
high. It has three to ten flowers, with blue or metallic green sepals and an
ascending stout spur, which are borne on erect spikes. The colour of this
arresting and beautiful flower can range from dark blue to an unusual
turquoise moss green shade. In the right conditions (in wetter cooler districts
such as Limuru and Kericho) this delphinium can be grown easily from seed
as a garden plant, but thrives best with strong competition from other bush-
like plants. It is found over a wide range in Kenya from 1,650–3,900m
(5,400–12,750ft). Flower: *c.* 3cm (1$\frac{1}{8}$in) across.

D. wellbyi is another beautiful and scented species with an open, wide flower
with blue to pale blue sepals and an ascending spur. It is common in Ethiopia
but in Kenya has only been recorded from upland grassland in the Nyambeni
Hills in Meru at *c.* 1,800m (6,000ft). Flower: 4.5cm (1$\frac{3}{4}$in) across.

D. leroyi is a rare species, very similar in appearance to *D. macroncentron* but
having white flowers. Altitude: 1,400–1,900m (4,600–6,250ft). Flower: *c.* 6cm
($\frac{1}{4}$in) across.

Ranunculus multifidus   **Plate 18** (114)
A perennial herb sometimes growing along the ground and propagating by
producing roots and shoots at the nodes or tip of the stem. It has numerous
yellow flowers and its leaves may be bi- or tri-sected. This is the commonest
'buttercup' in Kenya and is found at streamsides and growing as a weed at the
sides of tracks and roads in upland rain forest and moorland from
1,200–3,250m (4,000–10,750ft). Flower: 1cm ($\frac{3}{8}$in) across.

3. NYMPHAEACEAE
The Waterlily Family

A small family spread over the whole world with only some 35 species. They are aquatic perennials with floating leaves which may be heart shaped or have the stem attached to the lower surface. Sepals are free, petals may often pass gradually into the stamens, which are free. One genus is recorded in Kenya with three species.

Nymphaea caerulea (*N. capensis*)   **Plate 47** (304)
This waterlily, which is common in Kenya, is blue, but the centre of the ray-like flower is often orange-yellow tinged with red. Altitude range: 1–2,680m (3–9,000ft). Size of flower: 6–20cm ($2\frac{3}{8}$–$7\frac{3}{4}$in) across.

Nymphaea lotus   **Plate 8** (48)
A hairless waterlily with a tuberous rhizome and floating rounded leaves. Its flowers are white or cream. It is an uncommon species which can be found in Lake Victoria and Lake Jipe and has also been recorded in one or two pools in the coastal regions and in a marsh in Turkana, always below 1,200m (4,000ft). Flower: 10–18cm (4–7in) across.

4. HYDNORACEAE

This is a family of parasites which lack chlorophyll and grow on the roots of trees and shrubs by means of a pseudo-rhizome. The pseudo-rhizome is warty and may be simple or branched, round or angled; leaves and scale leaves are rounded. Flowers are large and solitary; the calyx fleshy and thick, three-lobed with the margins meeting; three to five stamens are inserted on the calyx tube and unite to form a ring around the stigma; anthers are numerous and lack stalks; the stigma is rudimentary or stalkless; the ovary is inferior and uni-locular, with many apical or parietal placentas, and ovules are numerous. Berry-like fruits are produced underground with a great many small seeds in a glutinous pulp. These plants reveal their presence by an evil smell although the unusual flower may not be detected. They are probably more common than is generally supposed. Two species are recorded in upland Kenya.

Hydnora abyssinica (*H. johannis*)   **Plate 29** (186)
A parasite with the underground pseudo-rhizome cylindrical or obscurely angled and completely covered with warts. The flower is large with a very strong unpleasant smell; the calyx is very fleshy and four-lobed with the inner surface cream to the apex and bright red and bristly below. It is usually found

27

growing on the roots of acacia trees at 90–1,500m (300–4,900ft). It is perhaps more common than is generally thought since it is only visible when in flower. Flower: 13–14cm (5–5½in) long.

5. PAPAVERACEAE

The Poppy Family

This is a rather small family of some 200 species found mainly in northern temperate areas. They often contain poisonous or medicinal substances, such as opium. The sap or juice is white or yellow. Solitary flowers on a long stalk have two to three sepals, four to six free petals, numerous stamens and a superior ovary with numerous ovules, fruit and capsules. The single species recorded in Kenya is introduced, not indigenous.

Argemone mexicana   **Plate 19** (124)
An erect herb with yellow flowers which produces yellow latex. Leaf bases circle the stem and the roughly oblong leaves are white-veined. It is a weed of waste dry places, roadsides and abandoned old cultivated ground which was introduced to East Africa from America under the name 'Mexican Poppy', from 1–1,800m (3–5,900ft). Flower: 5cm (2in) across.

6. CAPPARACEAE

A medium-sized, mainly tropical family of shrubs or small trees or, less often, herbs. Their leaves are alternate, simple or palmate. Flowers are bisexual and usually four in number with sepals, petals and stamens all free, the latter often numerous. The ovary is superior and usually stalked. Kenya has 65 species in ten genera, all but two of which are shrubs or small trees.

Capparis cartilaginea   **Plate 6** (41)
A spreading shrub, dull grey-green overall, which grows up to 2.4m (8ft). Its leaves are somewhat fleshy, ovate to rounded but with a sharp-pointed apex and with small backward-curving stipular spines. The flowers are white, ageing to mauve, with numerous stamens ageing to deep red. It is found in coastal areas and northern and northeastern regions on coral, rocks, sand and stony ground from sea level to 1,800m (6,000ft). Flower: *c*. 7cm (2¾in) across.

Cleome allamannii   **Plate 43** (276)
An annual, glandular or hairless, sticky plant with five to seven foliolate leaves and narrowly linear leaves, several of them with a conspicuous yellow patch. Its pink to magenta or mauve flowers form graceful racemes. It is

found in sandy or rocky soil in dry bushland where there is no cultivation, at 100–600m (300–2,000ft). Flower: petals 15–30mm ($\frac{1}{2}$–1$\frac{1}{8}$in) long.

Gynandropsis gynandra   **Plate 3** (17)
A tall annual with egg-shaped to elliptic leaflets. The flowers have white, pale pink or lilac petals. It is an easily recognisable weed, common on cultivated ground and by roadsides throughout Kenya from 1–2,400m (3–7,900ft). It is closely related to the preceding Cleome from which it can be distinguished by its larger and less graceful racemes. Flower: petals 10–20mm ($\frac{2}{5}$–$\frac{4}{5}$in) long.

Maerua edulis *(Courbonia glauca)*   **Plate 11** (70)
A bushy shrub which grows to 2.4m (8ft) having leathery, ovate or rounded leaves, their bases rounded or heart-shaped with an impressed pattern of veins on the underside. The solitary, axillary flowers are white with a wavy, feathery appearance, often closing slightly during the heat of the day. It is found at altitudes up to 1,850m (6,000ft). Freshly sliced pieces of root thrown into muddy water will clear the mud away. Flower: stamens 15–30mm ($\frac{5}{8}$–1$\frac{1}{8}$in) long.

Maerua kirkii   **Plate 8** (51)
A shrub or tree, growing to 4.5m (15ft) in height with erect branches. Its leathery leaves are obovate-oblong, 10cm (4in) long and 5cm (2in) wide with the apex rounded and sharply pointed and the base obtuse or subcordate, the upper surface rough and the lower covered with short hairs. Its green-white flowers, with black centres, are carried in dense, level-topped, many flowered racemes. It is found in semi-arid, warm districts from 100–1,300m (300–4,250ft). Flower: stamens *c.* 3cm (1$\frac{1}{8}$in) long.

Maerua subcordata *(Courbonia subcordata)*   **Plate 11** (71)
A much-branched shrub growing up to 2m (6ft). Its egg-shaped to rounded leaves are usually stiff and leathery with slightly prominent veining on both sides and more or less rounded or broadly wedge-shaped at the base. It is found in open grassland throughout Kenya at 100–1,200m (300–4,000ft). Its roots, like those of *M. edulis,* can be used for clearing muddy water. Colour of flower, greenish-yellow. Flower: filaments: *c.* 2cm ($\frac{3}{4}$in) long.

7.   CRASSULACEAE
The Stonecrop Family

A fairly large family of herbs or shrublets with succulent leaves, found mainly outside the tropics, usually in rather dry places. Their flowers are regular with four to five petals and sepals, either free or united, the calyx being persistent. The stamens are free and as many, or twice as many, as the petals. The four or

29

CRASSULACEAE

five fruit are free, or almost free; follicles and the seeds minute. There are 26 species in Kenya ranging through seven genera.

Crassula alba   **Plate 11** (68)
An erect herb, probably biennial, with a rosette of lanceolate, fleshy basal leaves and opposite leaves on the stem. Corymbs of closely clustered small white flowers are held on single stems springing from the base. A locally common plant of dry, rocky grassland at altitudes from 1,400–4,500m (4,600–14,750ft). It is found from north to south in the central highland areas and from the Cheranganis and Mau to Kajiado and Machakos. Each inflorescence: 5–10cm (2–4in) across.

C. alsinoides is a creeping or prostrate plant with elliptic, acute, unmarked leaves and solitary pink or white flowers which are borne on stems with linear leaves. It is locally common in temporary water pools around Nairobi. Flower: c. 6mm ($\frac{1}{4}$in) across.

C. granvikii is a soft perennial herb with a trailing base and tufted erect stems having linear leaves and a small tight bunch of pinkish flowers at the end. However, the leaves are often obtuse and not linear. It is a plant of considerable tolerance and is widespread at altitudes from 1,500–4,500m (4,900–14,750ft). At the higher altitudes the flowers are very small but in lowland forms can be very robust. Flower: c. 2–3mm (c. $\frac{1}{8}$in) across.

Crassula pentandra var. **phyturus**   **Plate 33** (213)
A low-growing soft but woody herb or plant trailing at the base with erect stems and succulent triangular-ovate or lanceolate leaves. The flowers are pinkish-white in dense axillary clusters. It is common in stony upland grassland over a wide area in nearly all the higher altitudes from 2,000–4,000m (6,600–13,100ft). The leafy shoots shown in the photograph are c. 6mm ($\frac{1}{4}$in) across.

Crassula sp. B   **Plate 30** (190)
A smooth, soft perennial herb with a trailing base and tufted erect stems with linear leaves and pink flowers. It has been reported only from the moorlands of Mt Elgon. Flower: c. 4mm (c. $\frac{1}{8}$in) across.

Kalanchoe densiflora   **Plate 15** (98)
An erect, hairless herb with a dense terminal corymb of yellow flowers. The stalked leaves, which are succulent, as are all Kalanchoe, are rounded to ovate and crenate. This is the commonest species of *Kalanchoe* and is found in disturbed places from 1,800–2,725m (6,000–9,000ft) in Elgon, Tinderet, Mau, Aberdares, Rift Valley, Embu, Machakos, Nairobi and Kajiado. Flower: c. 6mm ($\frac{1}{4}$in) across. Corymb: c. 10cm (4in) across.

30

K. lateritia is an ascending, glandular, down-covered, weak perennial with obovate, crenate, succulent leaves and rather small corymbs of bright red flowers. It is found in bushed grasslands in western Kenya in Kitale and Mumias districts and near the coast at altitudes up to 1,800m (5,900ft). Corolla tube: 9–12mm ($\frac{3}{8}$–$\frac{1}{2}$in) long. Flower: *c.* 15mm ($\frac{5}{8}$in) across.

Kalanchoe glaucescens   **Plate 25** (156)
An hairless perennial, trailing at the base and with erect stems, with obovate to ovate-elliptic, stalked leaves and small terminal corymbs of salmon-yellow to yellow flowers. It is a locally common plant found in stony bushland and recorded in Mumias, Narok, Baringo, Rift Valley and Machakos districts, from 400–2,000m (1,300–6,550ft). Corolla tube: *c.* 11mm ($\frac{3}{8}$in) long.

Kalanchoe lanceolata   **Plate 25** (155)
An erect, glandular, down-covered annual with a dense corymb of yellow to orange-red flowers. Its obovate to oblong, succulent leaves are entire or dentate and almost hairless. It grows to 1m ($3\frac{1}{4}$ft) in height and is locally common in dry country in Mt Elgon, Kitale, Mumias, Baringo, Rift Valley, Magadi, Machakos, Kajiado and Nairobi districts and Voi, Tsavo and inland coastal areas at altitudes slightly lower than *K. densiflora* from 200–2,100m (650–6,300ft). Flower: *c.* 11mm (*c.* $\frac{3}{8}$in) long.

Sedum ruwenzoriense*   **Plate 21** (136)
A trailing or erect, softly woody, small shrub with blunt cylindrical leaves and diffuse terminal cymes, yellow in colour. It is common in rock crevices in the moorland and lower alpine zones of the high Cheranganis, Aberdares and Mt Kenya at altitudes 3,050–3,900m (10,000–12,800ft). Flower: *c.* 9mm ($\frac{3}{8}$in) across.

S. meyeri-johannis is similar in all respects to *S. ruwenzoriense* except for its trailing habit. It is locally common as an epiphyte in highland mist zones on the Cheranganis, Aberdares, and Mau. Flower: *c.* 9mm ($\frac{3}{8}$in) across.

S. sp. A is a spreading herb with cylindrical acute leaves and yellow flowers in a corymbose terminal cyme. Found in stony soils at the upper forest levels on Mt Elgon.

8.   AIZOACEAE

This is a large family which is very well represented in South Africa, where there are hundreds of species related to *Mesembryanthemum*. They are annual or perennial herbs or shrublets, rarely shrubs. The leaves are simple and the flowers regular. There are no petals – what look like petals, as, for instance in Delosperma, are staminodes. There are 24 species in Kenya covering 13 genera.

Delosperma oehleri   **Plate 36** (231)
Originally described by Engler in 1909 from a specimen collected by Oehler
and Jaeger in northern Tanzania this species was not found again until
rediscovered by the photographer Peter Davey at 1,950m (6,400ft) on a
quartzitic hill in Narok district, when our photograph was taken. The
magenta colour of the petal-like staminoids was not recorded by the original
collectors. Flower: c. 12mm ($\frac{1}{2}$in) across.

D. nakurense is a shrubby low-growing perennial with unstalked fleshy, thick,
almost succulent leaves and pink, sometimes whitish, flowers. It likes to grow
in well-drained, crumbly rocky ground or among rocks in dry bush and
grassland at altitudes 1,500–2,100m (5,000–7,000ft) and is locally common in
parts of the Rift Valley and occasionally elsewhere. Flower: c. 2cm ($\frac{3}{4}$in)
across.

9. PORTULACACEAE

A rather small, mainly herbaceous family found in most parts of the world.
Its leaves are entire and often rather succulent. There are two sepals and five
(sometimes four or six) petals and from five to many stamens. The ovary is
superior and unilocular with one or more ovules attached to the base. There
are 11 species in Kenya ranging through four genera.

Portulaca kermesina   **Plate 16** (104)
A branched, fleshy perennial with slightly tapering leaves of a dull grey-green
and with numerous long (usually over 5mm/$\frac{3}{16}$in) hairs at the base of the leaf.
The usually solitary flowers are yellow. It is found in dry sandy or stony soils
in drier areas in the central and southern areas of Central and Rift Valley
districts from 1,200–2,200m (4,000–7,200ft). Flower: 1cm ($\frac{2}{5}$in) across.

P. foliosa is similar but has solitary flowers with pinkish sepals and yellow or
orange petals. The hairs at the leaf base are less numerous and shorter than
those of *P. kermesina*. It is fairly common at medium altitudes and has a wide
ecological tolerance. Flower: 5mm (c.$\frac{1}{5}$in) across.

Talinum portulacifolium   **Plate 43** (275)
A hairless perennial herb or small shrub with obovate to oblanceolate, fleshy
leaves and long terminal racemes of many flowers, purple to purple-pink;
pedicels recurved when in fruit. It is common on dry bushland at 9–1,650m
(30–5,900ft). Flower: c. 12mm ($\frac{1}{2}$in) across.
    Two other species of Talinum are found in Kenya. They are shorter, more
or less erect plants with yellow flowers.

10. POLYGONACEAE
The Dock Family

A medium-sized cosmopolitan family of herbs, shrubs or climbers and, very rarely, trees. Their leaves are usually alternate and the base often sheathing. Flowers are small and often unisexual; the regular, three- to six-lobed, perianth is often persistent (remaining after the normal time of withering); there are five to nine stamens and a superior ovary with only one ovule, fruit and nutlet. There are 28 species in Kenya distributed through seven genera.

Oxygonum sinuatum is an almost hairless annual with elliptic to oblanceolate or obovate leaves bearing one to three pairs of shallow lobed or entire pink flowers. It has never been recorded at the Coast and is found generally in waste places from 750–2,100m (2,500–7,000ft). It is the commonest *Oxygonum* and has unpleasant prickly fruits. Flower: *c.* 5mm (*c.* ¼in) across.

Polygonum afromontanum is an almost hairless scrambling or trailing plant with elliptic leaves and axillary clusters of few pink flowers. It is mentioned here as it is fairly common in the forest edges at the tree line on Mt Kenya and the Aberdares, from 2,100–3,150m (*c.* 7,000–10,300ft). Flower: *c.* 5mm (⅕in) across.

P. convolvulus is a climbing, twining, almost hairless annual herb with ovate acuminate or triangular hastate leaves and fascicles of pink flowers in racemes or borne axillary. It is an introduced species from Europe which is becoming noticeable in cultivated arable areas at 1,700–2,200m (5,500–7,200ft). Flower: *c.* 5mm (*c.* ⅕in) across.

P. pulchrum is a softly hairy perennial herb with narrow-lanceolate entire leaves, often with longitudinal undulations. The inflorescence is a raceme of one to five pink flowers. It is a locally common waterside plant and often found around artificial dams in most districts from 1,200–2,100m (4,000–7,000ft). Flower: *c.* 5mm (*c.* ⅕in) across.

P. salicifolium is an erect almost hairless annual with elliptic almost sessile leaves and a terminal group of slender interrupted racemes of pink or white flowers. It is a common waterside plant from 1,000–2,400m (3,300–8,000ft). Flower: *c.* 5mm (*c.* ¼) across.

P. senegalense is an erect variably hairy perennial like a soft shrub in general appearance; the stems are more or less covered with conspicuous slightly inflated brown sheaths. The leaves are lanceolate, acute, hairless or covered with dense white soft hairs, and the inflorescence is a raceme of pink or white flowers. It is a common herb of river and streamsides and marshes in almost all districts from 800–2,500m (2,600–8,200ft).

There are two distinct forms of this species between which intermediates occasionally occur; var. *senegalense* is almost hairless except for the glands while var. *albotomentosum* which is much less common is covered with dense soft white hairs. Flowers: *c.* 5mm ($\frac{1}{5}$in) across.

Rumex usambarensis   **Plate 26** (167)
A weak shrub, sometimes almost a climber, with oblong-elliptic leaves with a pointed top and outward pointing lobes at the base. The flowers are carried as a complex red panicle. It is a beautiful plant, common at 900–2,400m (3,000–7,900ft) which is often seen alongside roads and invading newly cleared woodland around Nairobi. Flower: panicle *c.* 7.5cm (3in) across.

R. abyssinica ranges from 730–3,300m (2,400–10,800ft). It prefers wetter places and in its lower altitudes is confined to stream banks and sides but higher in its range it replaces *R. usambarensis*. It has large leaves like those of the European docks; flowers green in colour. Flower: panicle up to 40cm (15$\frac{3}{4}$in) long; 25cm (9$\frac{3}{4}$in) wide.

R. bequaertii is the most common and widespread dock in Kenya. It has an erect raceme of greenish-brown clustered flowers and large leaves, like those of the two preceding species, and is also found in wetter places and at higher altitudes than *R. usambarensis* from 1,200–2,800m (4,000–9,200ft). Flower: panicle, 80cm (*c.* 30–32in) long; 30cm (*c.* 12in) wide.

R. ruwensoriensis is sparsely covered with short soft hairs. It has large oblong-lanceolate leaves, similar to those of European docks, and greenish-yellow to brownish-red flowers. It is the common dock above 2,250m (7,400ft) on the Aberdares and Mt Kenya and is often found along streamsides. Flower: panicle up to 40cm (15$\frac{3}{4}$in) long, 19cm (7$\frac{1}{2}$in) across.

11. PHYTOLACCACEAE

A rather small family which has alternate leaves and regular flowers. Ovaries may have one to many carpels, each with an ovule. Three species in two genera have been recorded in Kenya.

Phytolacca dodecandra   **Plate 6** (40)
A climbing, scrambling, or sometimes erect, hairless shrub with bluntly ovate-elliptic leaves and long, trailing terminal racemes of individually stalked, creamy-yellowish flowers. It is a local plant of bushland and cleared forest at 500–2,400m (1,650–7,850ft) and, although often found as a low

trailing shrub, it can be seen as a strong and tall climber in riverside forest. It is poisonous and responsible for many stock losses in dry seasons when grazing is scarce and the animals hungry. Inflorescence: *c.* 18mm ($\frac{3}{4}$in) across.

12. AMARANTHACEAE

A rather large family of herbs, shrublets or, occasionally lianes found throughout the tropics and warm-temperate regions. The small flowers are often surrounded by chaffy bracts. The perianth usually has five free, stiff, chaffy segments with a stamen opposite each segment uniting at the base to form a cup. The uni-locular ovary is superior and usually has one central, basal ovule. the fruit is usually dry, rarely fleshy. There are 60 species known in Kenya from all parts of the country except the high mountains, they belong to 20 different genera but are often hard to tell apart.

Centemopsis kirkii *(C. rubra)*　　　　　　　　**Plate 43** (278)
An erect, sparsely-downed annual or a short-lived perennial able to exist under a variety of conditions. It has linear sessile leaves and reddish spikes of two-flowered cymes. It is common in dry bushland at 100–1,900m (300–6,200ft) in eastern Kenya and recorded in Machakos, Nairobi and Kajiado. Inflorescence: *c.* 3cm (1$\frac{1}{8}$in) long.

Cyathula cylindrica　　　　　　　　　　　　**Plate 2** (13)
A scrambling perennial herb covered in soft hairs with lanceolate to ovate leaves and solitary, cylindrically uninterrupted, grey to slightly straw-coloured, terminal spikes. It is a rather uncommon plant found in the wetter high-level forests at 2,250–3,050m (7,500–10,000ft) but its trailing habit and usually hanging grey-silver racemes make it easy to identify. Inflorescence: *c.* 2cm ($\frac{3}{4}$in) diameter.

Cyathula polycephala *(C. schimperana)*　　　　**Plate 10** (67)
A hair-covered or woolly herb with ascending or erect stems and ovate-elliptic, heart-shaped or rounded leaves. The terminal inflorescence is leafless and crowded with pedunculate cymes which are spaced out so that each may develop into a separate straw-coloured ball. It is a common weed of upland grassland at 1,500–2,700m (5,000–9,000ft). Flower: a straw-coloured ball *c.* 22mm ($\frac{3}{4}$in) across.

Digera muricata　　　　　　　　　　　　　**Plate 37** (234)
An erect, often very tall annual which is usually unbranched below with linear to lanceolate leaves and long terminal spikes of purple flowers in the form of cymes with the sterile flowers of each cyme forming green wings. It is found in dry places, often on stony or sandy soil in grassland, at 900–1,500m (3,000–5,000ft) in districts such as Kisii, Baringo, Nanyuki, Machakos,

Magadi and Kajiado, and in dry low altitude areas such as the Northern Frontier districts. Flower: *c.* 4mm ($\frac{1}{6}$in) long.

Gomphrena celosioides　　　　　　　　　　　　　　　**Plate 11** (72)
A perennial herb covered with soft hairs and having prostrate or ascending branches and obovate to elliptic leaves. Its white terminal spikes are pedunculate. It came originally from South Africa but has spread as a weed during the present century in the tropics and subtropics and is now common at the sides of roads and paths over most of Kenya at altitudes up to 2,130m (7,000ft). Inflorescence: *c.* 12mm ($\frac{1}{2}$in) across.

Pupalia lappacea is very similar to *Cyathula* from which it differs in having alternately arranged cymes in the raceme, more highly developed sterile flowers with stellate hooks in fruit and no staminodes. It is an annual or perennial, prostrate, scrambling or erect herb with elliptic or ovate leaves and terminal, erect or pendulous racemes of grey-white flowers with well spaced, alternate cymes on short peduncles. It is widespread throughout Kenya at 10–1,900m (30–6,200ft) altitudes. It is an annoying plant which produces highly adhesive burrs, especially in dry country. They stick on all clothing. Flower (in dry country): sepal, 3.5–5mm ($\frac{1}{8}$–$\frac{1}{5}$in) long.

13. ZYGOPHYLLACEAE

A small family, recorded mainly in warm and arid regions, with leaves usually compound, flowers regular with four or five free sepals and petals and usually twice as many stamens. The ovary is superior with the fruit splitting into two or more one-seeded portions at maturity. There are some five species, covering three genera, known in Kenya.

Tribulus cistoides　　　　　　　　　　　　　　　**Plate 19** (123)
A creeping perennial with opposite and parapinnate leaves bearing four to seven oblong to oblong-lanceolate leaflets, with yellow or cream-coloured flowers. It is a plant of dry, arid and warm zones with sandy soils and found up to 1,500m (5,000ft) although rare at altitudes above 910m (3,000ft). Flower: 15–25mm ($\frac{5}{8}$–1in) across.

T. terrestris is much more widely spread and common at 320–1,950m (1,050–6,400ft) growing on sandy soils, waste ground near human habitations, roadsides and cultivated land. Its star-like yellow flowers project from the axils above the strictly opposite and oblong lanceolate leaves. The seed husks are spiked and irritatingly attach themselves to stockings. Amongst the Akamba people it used to be a test of manhood for young warriors to walk across a threshing floor covered with these spiked fruits without showing signs of pain. It is easily recognised along roadsides on sandy furrows and folds in National Parks such as Buffalo Springs and Tsavo West. Flower: 6–9mm ($\frac{1}{4}$–$\frac{3}{8}$in) across.

14. GERANIACEAE

The Cranesbill Family

A medium-sized, mainly herbaceous family containing only five genera, found in most temperate and subtropical regions but absent from the humid tropics. Its leaves are often palmately veined or lobed; sepals and petals are free and usually five in number, stamens twice as many; the ovary is superior, beaked, with three to five loculi and one or two pendulous ovules in each loculus. The fruit splits into several tailed, and usually single-seeded, mericarps. There are 14 species in Kenya belonging to three genera.

Geranium ocellatum   **Plate 41** (266)
An ascending, diffusely-branched, annual herb with spreading hairs or glands and rounded, palmatisect leaves. Its paired flowers are pink with dark, almost black-purple, centres. It is generally found in shade, as in caves, or along hill slopes or forest edges, but also as a weed in cultivated ground, and is recorded in Elgon, Tinderet, Rift Valley and Kitale at 1,650–2,800m (5,500 9,200ft). Flower: c. 14mm ($\frac{5}{8}$in) across.

Geranium aculeatum is a perennial trailing herb rooting at the nodes with sharp reflexed prickles and palmately lobed leaves. The flowers are almost always in pairs and white or mauve in colour. It is found in montane forests and moist places such as stream sides and marshy sides of valleys and sometimes as a weed in cultivated places from 1,900–2,700m (6,200 8,850ft). Flower: c. 16mm ($\frac{5}{8}$in) across).

Monsonia ovata   **Plate 14** (92)
An erect perennial plant with fleshy roots. The flowers, usually in pairs, are yellow or white and the leaves are opposite to each other on the stem. Found in open plains with acacia trees or wooded grassland on sandy and stony soils, in the Rift Valley, Machakos and Magadi districts at medium altitudes. Flower: c. 2cm ($\frac{3}{4}$in) across.

M. angustifolia is an annual with smaller mauve or white flowers which is widespread and often found on cultivated ground and damp grassland, at 400 2,200m (1,300–8,500ft). Flower: petals 7–15mm ($\frac{1}{4}$–$\frac{5}{8}$in) long.

M. longipes is a profusely branched perennial with up to five bright yellow or lemon flowers (also occasionally white) which appears to be limited to the Nairobi and Rift Valley areas, from 800–2,200m (2,600–8,500ft). Flower: petals 15–25mm ($\frac{5}{8}$–1in) long.

Pelargonium whytei   **Plate 41** (265)
A down-covered to almost hairless herb which lies along the ground except
for the upturned tip of the stem (and occasionally with groups of stems rising
at the same level). Its leaves are rounded, variously dissected and opposite.
There are two to five flowers per peduncle, usually with four petals which are
pink with red veins and seven antheriferous filaments. Although previously
only recorded with four petals this photograph, taken at 2,100m (6,900ft) on
the Gilgil West Road, clearly shows five petals. It is possible that, in certain
areas, the flower is variable in this respect. It is found in the drier parts of the
montane forest belt, in grassland regions and ericaceous habitats at
1,500–3,500m (4,900–12,500ft). Flower: *c.* 12mm ($\frac{1}{2}$in) across.

Pelargonium alchemilloides is a perennial herb covered with short soft hairs
with a slightly tuberous rootstock, and leaves alternate below and opposite
towards the apex, orbicular and five- to seven-lobed. The flowers, from five
rarely, and more normally seven, to as many as 16 per peduncle with five
white petals, though occasionally these are pink or dark red. It is found along
slopes of hills and mountains in grassland and savannah woodland extending
up to the edges of montane forest, at 1,400–2,500m (4,600–8,200ft).
Recorded in Elgon, Kitale, Rift Valley, Nanyuki, Machakos, Nairobi and
Kajiado. Flower: *c.* 2cm ($\frac{3}{4}$in) across.

15. OXALIDACEAE

A smallish family of herbs and in rare cases shrubs or trees which is well
represented in South Africa and South America. Leaves are alternate and
usually compound; flowers regular with five free sepals and petals, usually ten
stamens and with a superior ovary and a capsule fruit. There are nine species
in Kenya belonging to two genera.

Oxalis obliquifolia   **Plate 34** (218)
A bulbous plant with a vertical rhizome and the leaves trifoliolate in form. The
single pink or purple flowers on short erect stalks sometimes have a yellowish
base. Found in shallow soils at 750–2,900m (2,500–9,500ft), it occasionally
appears as a weed in cultivation and at roadsides in the Mau, Tinderet, Kitui,
Kisii, Baringo and Nairobi districts. Flower: 10–23mm ($\frac{3}{8}$–$\frac{7}{8}$in) long.

O. latifolia, the common oxalis, grows from small bulbils or runners and is a
common and pestilential weed in all gardens in East Africa but it is not
indigenous: it was introduced from America. The leaves and peduncle arise
directly from a small oval bulbil or from runners. The flowers are in five- to
over twenty-flowered pseudo-umbels and a light pink-purple in colour with a
green throat. The leaves are trifoliolate in form.

BALSAMINACEAE

16. BALSAMINACEAE

A family found in all tropical and subtropical regions, composed almost wholly of *Impatiens*, of which the best known are the 'Busy Lizzies'. There are 22 species in Kenya, all of the same genus.

Impatiens niamniamensis   **Plate 28** (181)
A hairless, woody herb which, if supported, can reach over 2m (6½ft) in height. Its leaves are ovate-lanceolate and its flowers are red or red and yellow with small petals and a big spur. A rare plant, it is found in wet forests in western Kenya at 1,350–1,800m (4,400–5,900ft). Flower: *c.* 14mm (⅝in) long.

Impatiens sodenii   **Plate 44** (287)
An erect, hairless herb 1–3m (3–10ft) tall, branched or unbranched from the base only with 10 to 15 elliptic to oblanceolate leaves in each whorl. Its nearly equal petals form a flat white, pink or slightly red, almost rounded outline. It is locally common in escarpment zones, near waterfalls and streams and in misty situations at 1,000–2,700m (3,250–8,800ft). Much transplanted into gardens it can now be found in many parts of Kenya. Flower: *c.* 35mm (1⅜in) across.

I. meruensis subsp. cruciata is a decumbent to erect perennial growing to *c.* 1m (3¼ft) tall, sometimes scrambling over supporting vegetation. The stems are simple to moderately branched usually densely covered with short soft hairs when young but becoming hairless when old. The leaves are long, slender generally hairless and spirally arranged; the flowers are pale to deep pink in colour, sometimes slightly mauvish, the upper petal of each lateral united pair with a slight purplish blotch towards the base. Common in Central and Southern Kenya in shaded places in forests or along pathways and the banks of rivers and streams at 1,100–3,630m (3,600–12,000ft). Flower: *c.* 25mm (1in) across (sometimes much reduced in size during drought).

I. pseudoviola is an annual or short lived perennial growing up to 30–40cm (11–16in) tall. Stems normally erect, simply or moderately branched and hairless, sometimes covered with fine hairs though becoming hairless below. Leaves are spirally arranged or occasionally subopposite, and ovate to ovate-rhomboid or ovate-elliptic, acute or shortly acuminate and the base shortly cuneate; hairless or covered with fine hairs above and below. The flower is single, though occasionally two or three together appear, violet pink or purplish in colour with a violet or yellow spot towards the base of the united lateral petals. It is found in damp shady places, upland rain forest amongst small herbs and mosses, sometimes on decaying tree trunks or stumps and the sides of streams and dry waterfalls. It is widespread in Central and Southern

39

Kenya, sometimes forming large colonies from 1,550–3,200m (5,100–10,500ft). Flower: *c*. 2cm (¾in) across.

17. THYMELAEACEAE

A small family, commonest in Africa, of perennial herbs with woody rootstock, shrublets, shrubs or small trees, usually with a tough fibrous bark. The flowers are regular, the lower part of the calyx remaining around the ovary in fruit (so that the fruit appears to be inferior), the upper part being tubular and petaloid. Small real petals appear at the mouth of the calyx tube or are absent. Fruit has one seed, an achene or drupe. There are 14 species in Kenya belonging to five genera.

Gnidia subcordata *(Englerodaphne subcordata)*   **Plate 7** (43)
A much-branched shrub growing to 3–5m (10–17ft). Its leaves are simple, alternate or opposite and usually small and without stipules. The white flowers are four in number in this species, although other *Gnidia* may have five. What appears to be a white tubular corolla is really the calyx, the eight apparent petals being eight small scales in its throat. It is found at 1,400–2,400m (4,600–7,900ft) in Tinderet, Mau, Aberdares, Loita Hills, Narok, Rift Valley, Nairobi, Kajiado and Nanyuki districts. Flower: 9–12mm (⅜–½in) long.

18. NYCTAGINACEAE

Herbs, shrubs or climbers, and, rarely, trees with alternate or opposite simple leaves without stipules. Inflorescences are usually cymose, with bracts; these are usually five-fused and petaloid sepals forming a sheath around the ovary in fruit; petals are rounded, stamens may be single or many, with the filaments often fused into a cup at the base and the anthers, with only two loculi; the ovary is single-celled with a style and capitate stigma and with one erect ovule. The fruit remains closed when ripe, the seed having some endosperm and a straight or curved embryo. There are 12 species in Kenya covering four genera.

Commicarpus pedunculosus   **Plate 39** (248)
A trailing plant or herb, sometimes with scrambling branches up to 50cm (20in) in length, with purple-magenta flowers. It is common in thickets and riverine areas in dry territories of eastern Kenya such as Narok, Rift Valley, Nanyuki, Embu, Machakos, Nairobi and Kajiado up to 2,100m (6,900ft). Inflorescence: *c*. 25mm (1in) across. Each flower: *c*. 5mm (¼in) across.

19. PROTEACEAE

A medium-sized family of evergreen trees, shrubs or plants with a woody rootstock which produce herbaceous branches every year, found mainly in southern Africa and Australia. They are hard leaved, have a perianth of four valvate segments, often united at the base, four stamens, a superior ovary and are usually uni-ovulate. Five species are known in Kenya, of two genera, the most common species preferring altitudes above 2,250m (7,500ft) and acid, often rocky, soils. The national emblem of South Africa is a protea and one species, *Grevillea robusta* the Silver Oak, is much planted in the Nairobi area, often as a windbreak in coffee plantations.

Protea kilimandscharica   **Plate 9** (57)
A relative of the better known South African Proteas. It grows up to $4\frac{1}{2}$m (15ft) in height at altitudes of 2,700–3,650m (9,000–12,000ft) in mountain savannah. The whitish-looking leaves and branches are hairless and smooth and the flowers white. Flower: up to 5cm (2in) across.

20. FLACOURTIACEAE

A medium-sized tropical or subtropical family of trees or shrubs. Their leaves are usually alternate and stipules often absent. Flowers are regular, stamens often numerous, the ovary superior and unilocular and the fruit a hard capsule or berry which remains closed when ripe. Kenyan species number 24 in 15 genera.

Oncoba routledgei   **Plate 8** (49)
A shrub or small tree up to 8m (26ft) tall with spiny branches and dark green, glossy leaves which are often wine red when young. The flowers are fine and waxy, rather like those of the Camellia. The leaves are elliptic or elliptic-oblong, with finely serrate margins and an acute apex. The fruit is large, woody and, when ripe, yellow and of 75mm (3in) diameter. Altitude range, 1,200–2,200m (3,950–7,200ft). Flower: *c*. 6cm ($2\frac{3}{8}$in) across.

O. spinosa is closely related to *O. routledgei* and has similar leaves and fruit but its flowers are not so fine and impressive. It is found in similar habitat to the preceding species at 20–1,800m (70–6,000ft).

21. CUCURBITACEAE
The Cucumber Family

A medium-sized family, which includes the gourds, cucumbers, marrows and melons, found throughout the tropics and subtropics but rare in temperate countries. These are prostrate or climbing herbs with tendrils, in rare cases they are rather woody. Their flowers are white, yellow or greenish and unisexual, the sexes often being borne on separate plants. The floral receptacle forms a cup or tube to the rim of which the five free sepals and five free or connate petals are attached. There are five basic stamens but they are often closely joined in pairs with the fifth free, giving the appearance of only three. The ovary is inferior and the fruit usually a berry but sometimes hard-shelled or, rarely, dry. There are 83 species in Kenya covering 23 genera.

Cucumis sp.   **Plate 19** (121)
Trailers or climbers without a swollen rootstalk and often with stiff hairs, tripalmate leaves and simple tendrils. The flowers are yellow and like those of the melon or cucumber, as are the leaves. The photograph shows an unidentified species from near the Chalbi Desert. Fruit: c. 55mm (2⅛in).

C. aculeatus is a common species with spiny, yellow, hooked hairs on stem ridges and is found in grassland or bushland at 1,100–2,200m (3,600–7,200ft) over much of eastern and central Kenya. Male flower: petal 6–9mm (¼–⅜in) long. Female flower: petal 8–13mm (5/16–½in) long.

C. prophetarum is a yellow-flowered perennial which is hairy but not spiny. It is common in bushland and semi-arid commiphora country at lower altitudes. Male flower: petals 5–6mm (c. ¼in) long. Female flower: petals 5–8mm (c. ¼in) long.

C. dipsaceus is also common in dry bushland at lower altitudes and can be distinguished by its stiff, almost prickly, spreading hairs and leaves which are hardly lobed at all. Male flower: petals 5–10mm (⅕–⅜in) long. Female flower: petals 6–15mm (¼–⅝in) long.

Peponium vogelii   **Plate 14** (90)
A climber growing locally in rocky places and on forest edges throughout Kenya. It survives in a wide variety of climatic and soil conditions. In the less humid areas its leaves are narrowly acute-lobed, in upland forest areas in zones of higher rainfall the leaf lobes are broad and obtuse with dense hairy stems. The flowers have white or pale yellow petals; the fruit bright red when ripe. It can be a short or a tall climber according to conditions and is found at altitudes 150–2,300m (500–7,500ft). Flower: 4–8cm (1½–3⅛in) across.

22. CACTACEAE

A medium-sized American family of stem succulents with only one genus in the Old World. Normally they have tufts of spines or bristly hairs and virtually no leaves. Petals and stamens are usually numerous, the ovary inferior and the fruit a berry. In Kenya there is only one native genus, *Rhipsalis*, but there are three or four introduced species of *Opuntia*.

Opuntia vulgaris   **Plate 24** (152)
Commonly known as the Prickly Pear and not truly wild in East Africa, this species was introduced from central America and is an escape from ranching country. In other countries, it has become a major menace, covering large tracts of land but in Kenya has generally been kept under control by local conditions. The flowers are yellow, often tipped with red, the fruit is the shape or size of a large egg, soft, green and covered with unpleasant prickles. Flower: 22–30mm ($\frac{7}{8}$–1$\frac{1}{8}$in) across.

23. OCHNACEAE

A rather small tropical and subtropical family of trees, shrubs and herbs with simple alternative leaves with rather distinctive stipules. The flowers are usually five in number with free sepals and petals and stamens often numerous. The superior ovary often has more or less free carpels. There are 15 species in Kenya belonging to five genera.

Ochna insculpta   **Plate 14** (93)
A shrub or small tree growing to 9m (30ft) with hairless, papery, oblong-elliptic leaves with their apex acuminate, margins finely-spiny denticulate and base broadly cuneate. Their veining is pinnate with the midrib pronounced beneath. Yellow flowers are carried in short, few-flowered racemes which terminate in very short branchlets. This species is found in several forests between 1,200–2,200m (4,000–7,200ft) and is especially common at Marsabit. Flower: 25mm (1in) across.

Ochna ovata   **Plate 17** (106)
A hairless shrub or, less often, a small tree. Leaves are ovate to oblong or lanceolate-elliptic with net-like venation, especially in age, their apex may be obtuse or acute, margins are evenly serrate and tend to be spiny. A few bright yellow-green flowers are grouped together in racemes on short axillary shoots which are often produced before the leaves have expanded. This species is common in less arid bushland and on the margins of forest around Nairobi and elsewhere in central Kenya at 600–1,900m (2,000–6,200ft), uncommon elsewhere. Flower: *c.* 12mm ($\frac{1}{2}$in) across.

24. COMBRETACEAE

A medium-sized tropical and subtropical family of trees, shrubs and woody
lianes with simple leaves lacking stipules. They have a calyx cleft into four or
five parts and a matching number or no petals. Stamens are as many, or twice
as many, as the sepals. The ovary is inferior and the feathery fruit, single-
seeded and often winged, remains closed when ripe. There are 36 species in
Kenya representing five genera; all but three species belong to the genus
Combretum, with opposite or whorled leaves, petals and four or five-winged
fruits, or to *Terminalia* with alternate or clustered leaves, no petals and flat-
winged fruits.

Combretum aculeatum   **Plate 9** (60)
A climbing and rambling shrub which grows up to 3m (10ft) in height with
zig-zag branches. Its leaves are alternate or sub-opposite, ovate and
covered in soft hairs. The white flowers have red anthers. It is found at the
coast and, in Masai and the Northern Frontier, often in thickets on dried out
swampy soils, and in all the rather dry parts of Kenya at 9–1,700m
(30–5,600ft). Flower: *c.* 11mm ($\frac{3}{8}$in) across.

Combretum mossambicense   **Plate 26** (161)
A shrub or loose climber covered in soft, downy hairs with ovate-elliptic,
rounded leaves and racemes of crowded flowers coloured pink, crimson,
green or creamy-pink. It is found in commiphora bushland, especially along
watercourses, at 600–1,200m (2,000–4,000ft). The photograph shows unripe
fruit which are *c.* 25mm (1in) long.

Combretum paniculatum   **Plate 26** (165)
A twining, woody climber with opposite leaves and hairless or down-covered
stems. Racemes of showy red flowers are borne in axillary panicles on
pendulous non-twining branches. This is a local and impressive plant whose
bright flowers can often be seen in the middle and upper branches of sparsely-
foliaged trees and found in or near riverine forest at altitudes below 1,300m
(6,000ft) but not on the coast. Inflorescence: branch illustrated *c.* 35mm
(1$\frac{3}{8}$in) long.

Terminalia prunioides   **Plate 10** (62)
A tall deciduous tree with grey, longitudinally fissured bark. Its branches
tend to appear in tables, or layers, like those of the Cedar of Lebanon. Its
leaves are obovate and wide with a wedge-shaped base, 5cm (2in) long and
25mm (1in) wide. The magnificent, but brief, display of white blossom is
reminiscent of cherry or plum blossom – hence the specific name meaning
'like prunes'. It is a native of the coast, Eastern and Northern provinces from
30–1,400m (100–4,600ft). Each spike of blossom: *c.* 56–80mm (2$\frac{1}{8}$–3$\frac{1}{8}$in) long.

25. HYPERICACEAE

The St John's Wort Family

A medium-sized family of trees, shrubs or herbs confined to the tropics, except for *Hypericum*, which mostly contain a yellow latex. Their four to five regular flowers are often yellow. Stamens are usually numerous and often united in bundles, the ovary superior and the three to five styles free or joined at the base. They include the tall shrubs or small trees with bright yellow flowers, common all over Kenya above 2,130m (7,000ft) which give off a strong scent like curry powder, c.f. *Hypericum revolutum*. Hypericaceae are now usually included in Guttiferae. There are 15 species in six genera recorded in Kenya.

Hypericum annulatum   **Plate 23** (147)
A member of the same family as the St John's Wort of European gardens, this minutely-haired perennial herb has ovate to lanceolate leaves and loose corymbs of flowers with much reduced glandular hairy bracts. In bud the flowers appear to be orange-red but when open are yellow. It is locally common on sandy grasslands at 1,150–2,400m (3,800–8,000ft) It is found in many districts: Tinderet, Mau, Aberdares and Mt Kenya in the higher altitudes and Rift Valley, Nanyuki, Machakos, Baringo and Kitale in the lower ones. Flower: *c.* 23mm ($\frac{7}{8}$in) across.

Hypericum revolutum   **Plate 21** (135)
A shrub or tree up to 12m (40ft) high. Its lanceolate to oblong-lanceolate leaves are up to 25mm (1in) long and 6mm ($\frac{3}{4}$in) broad, narrowing acutely to a clasping base with pinnate venation displaying linear and often translucent glands. Solitary yellow flowers are borne at the ends of branches, their stamens grouped in five bundles of about 30 each. It is a shrub of upland and dry evergreen forest bush. often riparian, at 1,930–3,290m (6,500–11,500ft). Flower: 4–5cm (1½ 2in) across.

26. TILIACEAE

The Lime Tree or Jute Family

A medium-sized family of trees, shrubs or herbs, often with hairs in radiating clusters, found throughout the tropics and subtropics, with *Tilia*, the Lime tree, alone in temperate countries. Leaves are alternate and stipulate, the calyx usually have five valvate sepals and the petals are free. Stamens are more numerous than the petals, usually free, and spirally arranged with the ovary superior. There are 45 species in Kenya covering five genera.

45

TILIACEAE

Grewia lilacina **Plate 34** (217)
A shrub growing up to 1.8m (6ft). The leaves are obovate-oblong, the apex rounded and the margins closely crenate-serrate. The flowers are solitary, generally appearing before the leaves and pink, lilac or magenta in colour. It is found at 750–1,200m (2,500–4,000ft) in warm semi-arid areas. Flower: *c.* 18mm (¾in) across.

Grewia similis **Plate 34** (216)
A shrub growing up to 1.8m (6ft) in height and sometimes climbing to 9m (30ft) or more. Its young shoots and inflorescence are down-covered. The leaves are elliptic, rounded to obtuse at the apex with margins finely serrulate and base rounded. The flowers are bright mauve, pink or magenta (very rarely white) in three to six or more flowered terminal and axillary inflorescences, appearing when the tree is in leaf. It is widespread in all areas with rainfall above 750mm (30in) from 600–2,100m (2,000–7,000ft) but does not occur in dry areas; in these, *G. Lilacina* will be found. In all species of *Grewia*, some or all of the hairs are stellate. Flower: *c.* 2cm (¾in) across.

Grewia tenax **Plate 5** (34)
A shrub up to 2m (6½ft) in height. Its leaves are rounded to obovate, usually about 8mm (⅓in) long but occasionally reaching 5cm (2in). Their apex is rounded and margins more or less coarsely dentate-crenate. One or two white flowers are borne on long, slender peduncles, jointed above the middle, green-yellow outside, white within with sepals 12mm (½in) long. It is found in dry acacia-commiphora bushland up to 1,500m (5,000ft) in coastal, northern and southern districts. Flower: 2cm (¾in) across.

Grewia villosa **Plate 29** (184)
A shrub up to 3m (10ft) in height with young parts covered with silky hairs. Its rounded, sometimes broadly elliptic leaves lack colour and are up to 10cm (4in) in diameter with the base often obliquely cordate, the margin serrate and the under-surface covered with grey down or weak, shaggy long hairs and with prominent veins. The dull yellow flowers with reddish veins have oblong petals, notched and much shorter than the sepals. The copper-coloured, hairy fruit is edible. Although nearly all the other species of Grewia have hermaphrodite flowers this species has male and female flowers on separate plants. The flower in the photograph is female. *G. villosa* is common in dry bush country up to 1,220m (4,000ft) at the coast and in northern and southern districts. Flower: *c.* 12mm (½in) across.

Triumfetta flavescens **Plate 17** (110)
A down-covered shrub with branches often densely covered with small black spots or dots. Its leaves are ovate to rounded, somewhat angular or slightly tri-lobed. The yellow flowers are loosely grouped in small clusters of cymes. It is a common plant in dry bush country generally in Kisii, Rift Valley,

Machakos and Kajiado, and especially in Magadi districts, at 910–1,830m (3,000–6,000ft). Flower: *c.* 15mm ($\frac{5}{8}$in) across.

Triumfetta macrophylla   Plate 18 (113)
An erect, much-branched, down-covered, woody herb or shrub with ovate or lanceolate and often undivided leaves and large sparsely-leafed terminal panicles of numerous cymes; flowers yellow in colour; capsules with hooked prickles are 3–7mm ($\frac{1}{8}$–$\frac{1}{4}$in) long. It varies considerably in the shape and size of leaves and in habit as it often behaves as a scrambler. It is the commonest *Triumfetta* in upland forest areas of Kenya and is often encountered at forest edges and along roadsides at 1,300–2,500m (4,250–8,200ft). Other species are much more common in lower, drier areas. Flower: *c.* 8mm ($\frac{3}{8}$in) across.

27. STERCULIACEAE

A small, medium-sized, tropical and subtropical family of trees, shrubs, shrublets and herbs, usually with some stellate hairs. Their leaves are alternate and usually have stipules. The three to five-lobed, valvate calyx is persistent. There may be up to five free petals, or none at all, forming a contorted corolla. Five to many stamens may be free or more or less united, with the ovary superior. There are 30 species in Kenya belonging to 10 genera.

Dombeya rotundifolia   Plate 9 (58)
A tree, growing to 2–4.5m (6–15ft) in height in the savannah and on forest edges, this *Dombeya* has feathery, rounded to broadly ovate leaves which are sometimes obscurely lobed, cordate at the base and often densely covered with stellate hairs. Flowers are borne in white or pinkish clusters and resemble cherry blossom. However, the petals persist for months and become brownish – in which state the tree is not very attractive. It prefers the altitude range 1,370–2,130m (4,500–6,900ft). Flower: *c.* 18mm ($\frac{3}{4}$in) across.

Melhania ovata is a grey canescent woody herb or low shrub with ovate or suborbicular leaves and axillary groups of one to three yellow flowers. A common roadside weed in dry grassland, where it can be mistaken for a Sida at first glance, it is recorded in Rift Valley, Embu, Magadi and Kajiado from 5–1,900m (15–6,200ft). Flower: *c.* 15mm ($\frac{5}{8}$in) across.

M. velutina is a rusty-coloured erect woody annual or short-lived perennial, covered with soft dense hairs. The leaves are ovate-elliptic with axillary groups of one to four yellow flowers. It is a common weed in the drier areas of Kenya, below 1,830m (6,000ft) and recorded in western Kenya and Kisii to Machakos, Nairobi and Kajiado in the east from 5–1,900m (15–6,200ft). Flower: *c.* 15mm ($\frac{5}{8}$in) across.

28. MALVACEAE

The Mallow, Hollyhock or Cotton Family

A large family of herbs or shrubs or, less often, trees, usually with stellate hairs, which is found throughout the world and includes the Hollyhock of British cottage gardens. Leaves are alternate, often palmately veined and have stipules. Flowers are regular, usually rather showy and often with an epicalyx of bracts outside the calyx. The five petals are usually attached to the base of the staminal tube and fall off as one unit. Stamens are numerous, their filaments united to form a tube around the styles. The ovary has several carpels which often separate in the fruiting stage (mericarps). There are nearly 70 species in 12 genera in Kenya. The four genera most often met may be distinguished as follows:-

Epicalyx absent:

Fruit splitting into mericarps:
Mericarps usually indehiscent, single-seeded *Sida*
Mericarps dehiscent, two to three-seeded, *Abutilon*
Fruit a capsule *Hibiscus*

Epicalyx present:

Fruit a capsule *Hibiscus*
Fruit of indehiscent mericarps *Pavonia*

Abutilon hirtum **Plate 23** (146)
An erect, sparsely branched, woody herb with ovate to rounded leaves. The orange-yellow flowers, grouped usually in loose terminal panicles at the end of the brown branches sometimes have a dark purple-red spot at the base. This species is found in dry acacia-commiphora bushland and grassland from 300–1,800m (1,000–6,000ft). Flower: *c.* 4cm (1½in) across.

Abutilon longicuspe **Plate 42** (267)
A perennial shrub with dense grey down on stems and leaf undersides, bearing rounded, cordate leaves. The flowers are rather smaller than *A. hirtum* and often hang down like crumpled bell tents. They are mauve, lavender or lilac with a darker centre and are borne in conical, terminal panicles. This is a common plant of upland forest edges at 1,500–2,750m (5,000–9,000ft) in Elgon, Tinderet, Mau, Aberdares, Mt Kenya, Narok, Machakos and Nairobi regions. Flower: *c.* 25mm (1in) in diameter.

Abutilon mauritianum **Plate 16** (100)
A soft, woody shrub with short, dense down and longer-spreading hairs, its leaves usually rounded and cordate. Its yellow-gold flowers are solitary with

more than 20 mericarps, each tapering acutely at the top into a hairy bristle and with the lateral hairless area also pointed at the top. This is the commonest of the genus generally found in Kenya at altitudes up to 2,000m (6,500ft). Flower: *c*. 3cm (1⅛in) across.

A. grandiflorum is very similar to *A. mauritianum*, with similar yellow-gold flowers, but lacking the long, spreading hairs. It is found in drier areas such as Kajiado, although it is also recorded from Mumias.

Hibiscus aethiopicus   Plate 21 (134)
A low-growing perennial herb with elliptic long leaves (in rare cases three-lobed) and single yellow flowers. It is a common plant which grows in shallow soil or hard clay grassland at 1,200–2,100m (4,000–7,000ft) throughout the central areas of Kenya from Kajiado and Narok to Kitale in the north-west. Its large, ornamental flowers appear only after the rains. Flower: 5cm (2in) across.

Hibiscus aponeurus   Plate 28 (180)
An erect, short-lived perennial with an often dense covering of yellowish to occasionally brownish hairs. Its leaves are oblong to ovate, its crimson flowers solitary and axillary. It is common in dry grassland throughout most of Kenya at 610–1,950m (2,000–6,400ft). Flower: 25mm (1in) across.

Hibiscus calyphyllus   Plate 23 (145)
A shrub with ovate-cordate, simple or shallowly three-lobed leaves. The yellow flowers, with a deep maroon patch at the base of each petal, are large and solitary on short pedicels. It is an occasional shrub in lowland dry woodland and evergreen woodland at 900–1,800m (3,000–6,000ft) over most of Kenya. Flower: *c*. 9cm (3½in) across.

Hibiscus cannabinus   Plate 36 (228)
A locally common erect annual. Its hairy stems also carry small spines. The leaves are rounded and three- to seven-lobed. The pendulous flowers are grey, grey-purple, purple or a bright yellow with a maroon or purple base and grouped in loose terminal racemes. They are similar to those of *H. calyphyllus* but tend to be slightly smaller and, when yellow with a maroon base, the maroon area is smaller and more central. They generally open most fully up to midday when they can be admired in their full glory. In the afternoon they hang limply. This species is found throughout Kenya at 600–2,100m (2,000–7,000ft) in dry grassland, although in the semi-arid areas it is often found on the edges of moist places and intermittent water-courses. Flower: *c*. 6cm (2⅜in) across.

Hibiscus flavifolius   Plate 9 (56)
This species is similar to *H. aponeurus* (above), but is more robust in growth

MALVACEAE

with ovate-rounded leaves and cream or white flowers. It is fairly common in dry rocky grassland at medium altitudes, 1,250–1,950m (4,100–6,400ft) in the Mumias, Narok, Rift Valley, Machakos and Kajiado districts. Flower: *c.* 22mm ($\frac{7}{8}$in) across.

Hibiscus fuscus   **Plate 9** (55)
An erect, sparsely-branched herb, woody up to 2–4m (6–13ft) in height, with brownish-black, stellate hairs on the stem, pedicels and calyx and colourless hairs on the leaves. The leaves are ovate-triangular, simple or (rarely) three-lobed. The white flowers are usually solitary and appear in the axils. It is a common plant in disturbed ground or old cultivated fields where it usually has small flowers. In natural rocky grassland, especially in the Rift Valley, it appears in a more branched form with flowers which are usually larger and pink or pale mauve in colour. It is found over the whole of Kenya at 1,250–2,300m (4,000–7,500ft). Flower: *c.* 3cm (1$\frac{1}{8}$in) across; large flowers: 4cm (1$\frac{1}{2}$in).

Hibiscus ludwigii *(H. macranthus)*   **Plate 13** (81)
Usually small with erect branches, this shrub is sometimes larger and trailing. It has sharp irritant hairs which break off in the skin. The generally solitary flowers are yellow with a maroon base. They droop and are never fully open. This is a common Hibiscus found at 1,520–2,440m (5,000–8,000ft), often in cleared forest grassland. Closed flower: *c.* 6cm (2$\frac{3}{8}$in) long.

Hibiscus lunariifolius   **Plate 16** (105)
Usually a small shrub with erect branches but sometimes longer and trailing, the whole plant is covered with frequent sharp irritant hairs which break off in the skin. Its leaves are ovate-triangular to pentagonal and sometimes obscurely lobed. The drooping flowers are in leafless racemes or solitary; their yellow petals have a maroon base and never fully open. It is similar to *H. ludwigii*, except that its leaves are usually smaller, and it is found in dry areas, especially in rocky country in Mumias, Kisii, Rift Valley, Magadi and Kajiado districts at 1,070–1,680m (3,250–5,250ft). Flower: *c.* 77mm (3in) across.

Hibiscus vitifolius   **Plate 9** (59)
Like the preceding two species this plant has irritant hairs, shallow yellow flowers with a contrasting maroon base and three to five lobes. In many districts at 1,220–2,440m (4,000–8,000ft) it is common at the edges of forest in areas with little rainfall. Flower: *c.* 6cm (2$\frac{3}{8}$in) across.

Pavonia patens   **Plate 17** (107)
A trailing or erect shrub covered with stellate downy hairs. Leaves are ovate to rounded-cordate and flowers solitary. The petals are yellow, sometimes with a dark spot at the base within. This is a very variable plant with a wide

ecological tolerance from commiphora woodland to upland wet forest edges. At lower altitudes the fruit is warty; at the higher smooth. It is found throughout Kenya at 91–2,300m (300–7,500ft). Flower: corolla c. 3cm ($1\frac{1}{8}$in) across.

Pavonia urens   **Plate 35** (220)
A soft, usually rather hairy, shrub which grows on the edges of upland forest and along the sides of streams and water-courses in drier areas. The flowers are clustered or single and vary in colour from pink to mauve and white. It is widespread at 1,220–2,740m (4,000–9,000ft). Strong, flexible ropes are made from the stems and branches by some of Kenya's pastoral people. Flower: 2–4cm ($\frac{3}{4}$–$1\frac{5}{8}$in) across.

Pavonia zeylonica   **Plate 14** (91)
A short-lived perennial or annual covered with hairs on all its parts. The leaves are rounded and three- to five-lobed. Its solitary flowers are pale yellow or cream. It is common in dry acacia-commiphora bushland at 45–1,070m (150–3,500ft) after rains. Flower: c. 15mm ($\frac{5}{8}$in) across.

Sida cuneifolia is an erect or spreading shrub with oblanceolate to narrowly-obtriangular to almost linear oblong leaves and solitary yellow flowers. It is common in dry grasslands, forming wiry bushes especially in overgrazed land. It is a very variable species and common everywhere from 100–3,000m (300–9,800ft). Flower: 9mm (c. $\frac{3}{8}$in) across.

S. rhombifolia is an erect, short-lived perennial with ovate-elliptic or rhombic leaves and yellow flowers in axillary racemes, though sometimes solitary. It is common and widespread, especially in places disturbed by man from 900–2,500m (2,950–8,200ft). Flower: c. 1cm (c. $\frac{3}{8}$in) across.

29. MALPIGHIACEAE

A small to medium-sized, tropical or subtropical family of woody climbers or less often, trees, shrubs or shrublets, mainly in America. Flowers are mostly regular and five in number with ten stamens and a superior ovary, usually trilocular. Styles are free or joined below. There are ten species in Kenya belonging to five genera.

Caucanthus albidus   **Plate 10** (61)
An erect or scrambling shrub with masses of sweetly-scented creamy white flowers which are often conspicuous in dry bushland after rain at altitudes of 180–600m (600–2,000ft). The winged fruit is distributed by the small whirlwinds or 'dust devils' which are frequent in this dry country and travel across it. Flower: c. 1cm ($\frac{2}{5}$in) across.

30. EUPHORBIACEAE

A very large, mainly tropical family of herbs, shrubs and trees. Leaves are usually stipulate, flowers unisexual, monoecious or dioecious. Petals are usually absent and the ovary trilocular. There are about 185 species in Kenya belonging to 39 genera.

Acalypha volkensii   **Plate 32** (205)
A loose trailing, softly woody plant with simple, serrate leaves and very narrow, axillary racemes of hairless red flowers. Common in upland grassland and forest margins at 800–2,700m (2,600–8,850ft). Flower: *c.* 3cm (1⅛in) across.

Euphorbia graciliramea   **Plate 25** (160)
A small prostrate herb with succulent cylindrical stems which grows from a woody rootstock. The brownish-yellow flowers have a faint purplish tinge and on each spine shield form two small spines and one large one. Locally common at altitudes of 900–1,650m (3,000–5,500ft) in the Narok, Rift Valley, Magadi, Nanyuki, Nairobi and Kajiado districts, it is also seen in the Masai Mara area. Each flower: (really a group of reduced flowers) *c.* 7mm (¼in) across.

Euphorbia kibwezensis *(E. nyikae)*   **Plate 26** (166)
A tree growing to 6m (20ft) or more with a cylindrical bole surmounted by a crown of curved ascending limbs or branches. The branches are grey-green and hairless, three- to four-angled, though occasionally flat, and constricted into segments of varied shape, 5–20cm (2–8in) long and 5–7.5cm (2–3in) in diameter, the angles wing-like, very thin and unevenly toothed and wavy. The flowering eyes are yellow and carried in pairs, just above the spine. The fruit or seed is red. This is a tree of semi-arid and arid areas in thicket bush and on rocky shores. It is sometimes found in dry situations near coast or lake shores. Altitude range 400–1,600m (1,300–5,250ft). Flowers in cluster: 6–7mm (⅕–¼in) across. Fruit: *c.* 20mm (¾in) across.

Note. All species of Euphorbia contain a white latex. This contains some rubber and may yield a substitute for petrol but causes intense lasting pain if it reaches the eyes. Affected eyes should be bathed in milk.

31. ROSACEAE
The Rose Family

A large family, found mainly in temperate regions. Leaves are usually alternate, often divided and with stipules present. Flowers are usually perigynous with the receptacle forming a cup or saucer around the pistil with

ROSACEAE & LEGUMINOSAE

the sepals, petals and stamens attached to its rim, or occasionally to the inferior ovary. Petals are free and stamens often numerous and there may be one or many, more-or-less free carpels. In Kenya 29 species belonging to nine different genera are found at altitudes above 1,000m (3,280ft).

Alchemilla fischeri   **Plate 15** (30)
A trailing herb with rosettes of deeply-lobed hairy leaves, lobes obovate and rounded at the apex. The inflorescence is a small panicle formed of small masses of nearly stalkless, whitish flowers. It is common in philippis woodland on the Aberdares and Mt Kenya at altitudes 2,350–3,380m (7,600–11,100ft). Leaves: *c*. 10cm (4in) across. Flower: 2mm ($\frac{1}{10}$in) across.

Hagenia abyssinica   **Plate 30** (194)
A tree which grows to a height of about 15m (50ft) in the margins of high altitude forest areas. Its bark is dark red-brown and flakes off irregularly; leaves reddish when young and flowers pendant. The female flower is reddish and more bulky than the male which is orange-buff or white with a more plume-like appearance. The inflorescence of this tree yields a powerful medicine for dealing with intestinal worms and in Ethiopia, where the tree is called Kosso, is much valued on this account. Inflorescence: 30–50cm (12–20in) long.

Rubus steudneri   **Plate 33** (212)
A densely-haired scrambler with trifoliolate leaves and pink to purple flowers with large petals. It is allied to the Blackberry of northern Europe, although the berry is a deep orange to plum-coloured red drupe and hairless. It is locally common in undergrowth in forest clearings and edges at 1,800–3,050m (6,000–10,000ft). Flower: *c*. 18mm ($\frac{3}{4}$in) across.

R. pinnatus inhabits much the same altitude in bamboo and rain forest. The leaves are pinnate, the flowers pink and the fruit black. The petals are often absent and if present, much shorter than the calyx. It is found at 2,400–3,000m (7,850–9,850ft). Flower: 12–20mm ($\frac{1}{2}$–$\frac{3}{4}$in) across.

32–34. LEGUMINOSAE (Fabaceae)

An enormous group of trees, shrubs, lianes and herbs found throughout the world. They are sometimes treated as an order containing three families but it is now more usual to consider them as a family with three subfamilies, Caesalpinioideae, Papilionoideae and Mimosoideae. Their leaves are almost always alternate and stipule and usually compound. Flowers are perigynous as in the Rosaceae and the fruit in the form of one, or very rarely more than one, free carpel which usually splits lengthwise into two valves, occasionally splitting transversely or indehiscent.

53

32. Caesalpinioideae

Mainly tropical trees or shrubs or rarely herbs. Leaves pinnate, rarely simple or bi-pinnate. Flowers zygomorphic, the upper petal inside the two lateral petals. Stamens usually free, often fewer or more than ten. 65 species in 21 genera in Kenya, nearly half of them are *Cassia*.

Bauhinia taitensis   **Plate 12** (76)
A shrub which grows to a height of 1.7m (5ft) with many stems and branches. Its rough bark is grey-brown and its small leaves are covered with down. Yellowish, creamy white flowers are produced in great numbers. It is found at 300–1,070m (1,000–3,500ft) in Machakos, Taita Hills and Northern Province. Flower: petals 13–24mm ($\frac{1}{2}$–1in) long.

B. tomentosa is an erect shrub growing up to 7.5m (25ft) in height. Its leaves are bilobed up to 635mm ($2\frac{1}{2}$in) wide, hairless or with minute soft hairs beneath, rounded at the apex with three main nerves in each lobe. The flowers are large, solitary or in axillary pairs, or sometimes in inflorescences of a few flowers together with a corolla of five petals up to 5cm (2in) long, all yellow in colour but sometimes with the upper petal having a maroon or purple spot at the base. It is found in the coast, central and northern districts at altitudes of 20–1,600m (65–5,200ft). Flower: 3–4cm ($1\frac{1}{8}$–$1\frac{1}{2}$in) across.

Cassia abbreviata   **Plate 16** (101)
A small, many-branched tree which grows to 7.5m (25ft) in height. Leaves are to 25cm (10in) long, consist of five to thirteen pairs of leaflets, each up to 4cm ($1\frac{1}{2}$in) long, elliptic or elliptic-long, apex rounded or emarginate. Fragrant golden-yellow flowers form terminal and axillary corymbs with persistent and conspicuous bracts. Pedicels are 63mm ($2\frac{1}{2}$in) long, petals 12mm ($\frac{1}{2}$in) and the filaments of the three larger stamens are dilated at the base. It is found in some coastal areas and in dry bushland from 50–1,000m (160–3,250ft).

Cassia didymobotrya   **Plate 20** (130)
A poisonous shrub or small tree which grows to 6.5m (20ft) in height. It is common everywhere in Kenya from 600–2,100m (2,000–7,000ft) and often seen, especially along or just beyond the ditches and depressions at the sides of roads. The bright yellow flowers appear to have a dark blob at the top where the still unfolded buds show brown. The roots provide an antidote to the poison produced by the stem and leaves. The Maasai use an infusion of the leaves as a purgative and the hard stems can be used to produce fire by rotating them between the hands against a softer wood in Boy Scout fashion. The spark can be encouraged with the breath and used to ignite dry kindling such as the soft lining of a weaver bird's nest. Flower: c. 3cm ($1\frac{1}{8}$in) across.

Cassia grantii   **Plate 22** (142)
A prostrate perennial which produces annual branches from woody roots.
Oblong leaves bear six to eleven pairs of large, oblong, blunt leaflets. The
yellow flowers often have a tinge of red or a red stripe on the outside of the
unopened or semi-open bud. Found in dry bushland at 1,200–1,800m
(4,000–6,000ft), though on Mt Kenya it has also been recorded at 2,100m
(7,000ft) and higher. Flower: *c.* 12mm ($\frac{1}{2}$in) long.

Cassia singueana   **Plate 13** (82)
A tree which grows up to 6m (20ft) with scaly and fissured grey or brown
bark. Masses of glorious golden-yellow flowers are produced on short
corymbose racemes which are clustered at the end of the branches. It is found
from sea level to 1,980m (6,500ft) all over the warmer medium rainfall
savannah areas and often seen in both East and West Tsavo. Flower: *c.*
36mm ($1\frac{3}{8}$in) across.

Delonix elata   **Plate 24** (150)
A tree of the dry bushland, usually 4.5–6m (15–20ft) high, although
sometimes up to 12m (40ft), with a spreading crown and drooping branches.
The shining, grey-buff bark is smooth. The bi-pinnate leaves are 7.5–15cm
(3–6in) long, the pinnae usually in four to six pairs and the leaflets in 10–14
pairs, oblong to oblanceolate-oblong and 6–12mm ($\frac{1}{4}$–$\frac{1}{2}$in) long. The corymb
is terminal or comes from the upper axils with only one flower in an
inflorescence open at a time. The white corolla fades to a creamy yellow and
the staminal filaments are pale brown to reddish and hairy at the base. It is
found in altitude range 450–1,000m (1,500–3,300ft). Flower: stamen filaments 6–11mm ($\frac{1}{4}$–$\frac{3}{8}$in) long.

Tylosema fassoglense   **Plate 18** (117)
A large trailing climber with tendrils and cordate, notched leaves. Its
conspicuous flowers have crinkled petals and range from yellow to pink. It is
locally common in hot country with a medium rainfall 400–500mm (15–20in)
per annum. Recorded in Elgon, Cheranganis, Kitale, Mumias, Kisii, Narok,
Nanyuki and Machakos districts at 90–1,800m (300–5,900ft). Flower: 55mm
($2\frac{1}{8}$in) across.

33. Papilionoideae (Faboideae) The Pea Family

Tropical and temperate herbs, shrublets, shrubs and trees. Their leaves are
most commonly tri-foliolate but are also often pinnate and sometimes simple
or palmate. Flowers are zygomorphic, the upper (adaxial) petal or 'standard'
outside the two lateral petals ('wings') which in turn enclose the two lower
petals, which are more or less united to form the 'keel'. There are ten stamens,
variously united or, more often, free. In Kenya there are 450 species of this
family covering 75 genera. In so large a family, it is helpful to recognise tribes.

The chief tribe in most tropical countries is centred around *Phaseolus* – which includes the Scarlet runner and other beans. Members of this tribe are often twiners and nearly always have pinnately tri-foliolate leaves, often with stipels.

Calpurnia aurea *(C. subdecandra)* is a small tree with imparipinnate leaves about 25cm (10in) long with six to 14 pairs of elliptic to long leaflets rounded at the apex. The fruits are carried in membraneous pods 15cm (6in) long which remain on the tree for a long time. It is common in forests on the Mau, the Laikipia Escarpment and in the Rift Valley from 2,100–2,500m (7,000–8,000ft) though along streams it descends to lower altitudes, e.g. 1,500m (4,900ft) at Hippo Pool in the Nairobi National Park. Flower: *c.* 25mm (1in) across.

Clitoria ternatea   **Plate 46** (299)
A very beautiful climber with pale to bright blue flowers which grow singly or in pairs from the axils of the leaves which are pinnate with five to seven leaflets. It may be covered in blossoms, which produce flat green seed pods, and thrives in warm, dry bushland conditions in the Magadi, Nanyuki, Embu, Machakos and Kajiado districts at altitudes below 1,500m (5,000ft). Flower: 15–35mm ($\frac{5}{8}$–$1\frac{3}{8}$in) across.

Crotalaria agatiflora   **Plate 15** (95)
There are three races of this handsome shrub or small tree, all having attractive greenish-yellow flowers which, on first sight, look like those of a giant lupin. They are:

1. A high altitude type, growing from 2,300–3,200m (7,000–10,500ft) in areas of good rainfall where it is common in mixed forest and on the edges of grassland glades in forest country. This striking and attractive tree-like shrub is the form most likely to be observed. It can exceed 4m (13ft) in height and has elliptic lanceolate leaves. Its long, dark brown seed pods are oval shaped and hang in clusters from the stem, each 7.5–10cm (3–4in) long. It is found in areas such as Elgon, Tinderet, Mau, Loita Hills, Aberdares, Mt Kenya and Rift Valley.
2. A medium altitude form, smaller in size and hairy, found in grassland and bushland at an altitude of 1,800–2,100m (6,000–7,000ft) in much the same areas as the high altitude type.
3. A smaller and more woody form which prefers open spaces at 1,500–2,400m (5,000–8,000ft) in the Mau, Aberdares, Rift Valley, Machakos and Nairobi districts. Flower: *c.* 45mm ($1\frac{3}{4}$in) long.

At least 67 different species of Crotalaria have been identified in Kenya, nearly all of them with yellow flowers (and less commonly with blue or white) on erect spikes which resemble those of lupins. Their stems are often hairy and species can be found at every altitude, often in great drifts or clumps

PAPILIONOIDEAE

along roadsides. In some districts baskets are woven from the fibres of the branches and stems. (See species below).

Crotalaria axillaris   **Plate 23** (143)
A shrub or woody herb of upland areas of Kenya. It is coarsely hairy with elliptic leaflets and clusters of yellow flowers in the axils. The keel, which conceals the stamens and styles, is as long as the wings, (the two side petals,) and rounded with a twisted beak. The seed pod is oblong to club-shaped. This plant is found at 1,300–2,300m (4,400–7,500ft) and recorded in the Aberdares, Mt Kenya, Rift Valley, Embu, Machakos, Nairobi and Kajiado districts, in dry evergreen forest and derived communities persisting in disturbed places. Flower: keel 15–18mm ($\frac{5}{8}$–$\frac{3}{4}$in) long, pod 45mm (1$\frac{3}{4}$in) long, 6–12mm ($\frac{1}{4}$–$\frac{1}{2}$in) across.

Crotalaria cleomifolia   **Plate 12** (77)
A striking shrubby perennial which grows to 1–4.5m (3–14$\frac{1}{2}$ft) tall. It has three- to five-foliolate leaves, elliptic leaflets and long racemes of bright yellow flowers faintly lined with red. The calyx has long bracteoles from its blunt base. The standard, upper petal is elliptic; the keel is rounded with a narrow, slightly incurved beak and much larger than the wings. Locally common by streams and swamps or in grassland and bushland near forest at 1,200–2,300m (3,900–7,550ft), it is generally recognised by its predominately five-foliolate leaves. Recorded in Elgon, Tinderet, Mau, Aberdares, Nyambeni, Kitale, Western Kenya and Machakos. Flower: c. 16mm ($\frac{5}{8}$in) long.

Crotalaria laburnifolia   **Plate 18** (112)
A robust, semi-soft plant with lupin or pea-like yellow flowers, often speckled reddish-brown, hanging loosely from their stems. It is widespread throughout Kenya in bushland and wooded grassland from sea level to 1,830m (6,000ft). The specimen illustrated was photographed in the Mathews Range, an indication of how widely it is distributed.
There are also two subspecies:–

C. l. subsp. **eldomae** has a more diffuse habit, with small leaflets and racemes with fewer yellow flowers. It grows in dry places and volcanic soils in Rift Valley, Magadi and Kajiado.

C. l. subsp. **laburnifolia**, Elgon race, is found at 1,520–2,380m (5,000–7,500ft) in Kitale and Mumias, also with yellow flowers. Flower: 22–30mm ($\frac{7}{8}$–1$\frac{1}{4}$in) long.

Crotalaria lebrunii   **Plate 19** (120)
This *Crotalaria* has flowers similar to *C. laburnifolia* but the seed pods are pointed and elliptic and it is mainly confined to forest edges at 2,130–2,350m (7,000–7,700ft) in the Aberdares, Mt Kenya and Nyambeni Hills. It can be seen near the forest lodge, the Ark. Flower: 25–30mm (1–1$\frac{1}{4}$in) long.

57

Crotalaria mauensis   **Plate 13** (83)
A robust, bushy herb or shrub growing to 1.8m (6ft) in height, covered with short brown hairs and with elliptic leaflets. Yellow flowers form rather dense racemes with a broadly-lobed calyx the same length as the chubby corolla (12–15mm, $\frac{1}{2}$–$\frac{5}{8}$in). It is found at altitudes 1,680–2,300m (5,400–7,500ft) from Machakos district in the east to Mumias in the west. Flower: standard 12–15mm ($\frac{1}{2}$–$\frac{5}{8}$in) long.

Desmodium repandum is a loosely branched herb with trifoliolate leaves bearing ovate to rhomboid leaflets; the reddish-pink flowers are borne in terminal panicles or pseudo-racemes. It is common in shade in forest, particularly along streams and pathways where its sticky fruits easily attach themselves to clothing, and recorded in Elgon, Tinderet, Mau, Aberdares, Kitale and Western Kenya at 1,500–2,800m (4,900–9,200ft). Flower: *c.* 18mm (*c.* $\frac{3}{4}$in) across.

Eriosema psoraleoides   **Plate 13** (84)
A downy, erect, woody shrub with rounded oblanceolate to cuneate leaflets and long axillary racemes of yellow flowers. It is locally common in disturbed rocky bushland from sea level to 2,000m (6,500ft). Flowers: 7–14mm ($\frac{1}{4}$–$\frac{1}{2}$in) across.
  The flowers of all species of *Eriosema* are yellow or yellow and brown with the exception of *E. cordifolium*. All have a two-seeded pod.

E. cordifolium has pink and yellow flowers. It is found in short upland grassland above 2,290m (7,500ft) on Tinderet and Elgon. Flower: 5–6mm (*c.* $\frac{1}{4}$in) long.

E. glomeratum has yellow flowers on short stalks and leaves mostly elliptical. It is a spreading, hairy herb and common at the coast and up to 900m (2,950ft) but rare up-country. Flower: 6–8.5mm ($\frac{1}{4}$–$\frac{1}{3}$in) long.

E. jurionum is a hairy species with elliptic leaves and ovoid spikes which have brown and yellow flowers. It is locally common at upland forest edges, from 2,000–2,800m (6,550–9,200ft). Flower: 5–8mm ($\frac{1}{4}$–$\frac{1}{3}$in) long.

E. nutans has lanceolate to elliptic leaflets. Its dense cylindrical racemes of yellow flowers look a little like a delicate column of lupin flowers. It is common in wooded grassland and forest edges in the Aberdares, Tinderet, Kitale, Rift Valley and Machakos districts from 1,200–2,400m (3,900–7,900ft). Flower: corolla 7mm (*c.* $\frac{1}{4}$in) long.

E. robustum has very hairy yellow flowers and is common in wooded grassland around Kitale and also found in the Aberdares, Rift Valley and Kisii at altitudes of 1,500–2,200m (4,900–7,200ft). Flower: *c.* 13mm (*c.* $\frac{1}{2}$in) long and 9mm (*c.* $\frac{3}{8}$in) wide.

PAPILIONOIDEAE

Erythrina abyssinica   **Plate 26** (162)
A deciduous tree growing up to 12m (40ft) in savannah or scrub land and
partial to laterite or rocky subsoils. The leaves are tri-foliolate with their stalks
covered with grey hairs when young, becoming hairless, or nearly so, as they
grow older. The leaflets are generally sparingly downed above and densely
covered with grey hair below. They are broadly ovate to rhomboid or
rounded with the terminal leaflet up to 20cm (8in) broad, usually broader
than long, blunt at the apex and broadly rounded to cordate at the base. The
branches are stout, armed with strongly recurved thorns and densely haired
when young. The flowers appear before the leaves open and are a bright coral
red to scarlet in colour. They form dense, erect, poker-like inflorescences.
This plant can be found in most parts of Kenya having a rainfall of 75mm
(35in) or more, at altitudes 200–2,100m (600–6,800ft), but not in dense forest.
It can be propagated from cuttings. Inflorescence: 5–15cm (2–6in) long.

Indigofera arrecta is a stout rather woody herb 1–2m ($3\frac{1}{4}$–$6\frac{1}{2}$ft) tall though
occasionally it can be 3m (nearly 10ft) in height. The leaves are up to 6cm
($2\frac{2}{5}$in) long with seven to 17 leaflets each of which is up to 20mm (c. $\frac{3}{4}$in) long.
The inflorescence is a many-flowered raceme up to 5cm (2in) long but usually
shorter than this; the flowers are red inside when open but the outside is
covered with short stiff brown hairs; the seed pod is deflexed and straight and
brown in colour, 12–17mm (c. $\frac{1}{2}$–$\frac{2}{3}$in) long with 4 to 8 seeds. The flowers at
higher altitudes are rather larger in size with a greater proportion of brown or
black hairs than those at lower altitudes. It is found in grassland, bushland
and forest margins up to 2,500m (8,100ft) in almost every district. Flower:
corolla c. 5mm ($\frac{3}{16}$in) long.

I. atriceps is a coarse branching sub-erect herb up to 2m ($6\frac{1}{2}$ft) tall, covered
with short bristles often dark or black in colour except for those on the
leaflets. The seed pods always have pale or reddish glandular hairs on them
and are up to 10mm ($\frac{2}{3}$in) long. The leaf rachis is 1–6cm ($\frac{2}{5}$–$2\frac{2}{3}$in) long with
leaflets nine to 13 in number. The inflorescence is a dense many-flowered
pedunculate raceme on a peduncle and the corolla is a dull red in colour. This
is a very variable species and is found in moist grassland, in bracken and at
the edges of Montane forest from 1,100–2,500m (3,600–8,100ft) almost
everywhere within its zone in Kenya. Flower: corolla c. 7mm (c. $\frac{1}{4}$–$\frac{5}{16}$in) long.

I. brevicalyx is a spreading, sparsely appressed-strigulose perennial with five
to 13 leaflets each with three translucent blisters, one beneath each side and
one at the tip. The inflorescence is a two- to three-flowered raceme up to 5cm
(2in) long, brick red in colour. Each lobe of the calyx which can be up to
1.5mm ($\frac{1}{16}$in) long has a blister. It is found in short grassland from
1,400–2,000m (4,700–7,000ft) almost everywhere in this altitude zone though
it is not recorded in Western Kenya. Flower: corolla 8mm ($\frac{5}{16}$in) long.

59

PAPILIONOIDEAE

I. spicata is a prostrate or ascending perennial with ridges but more or less flattened stems. The leaves are up to 4 or 5cm (*c.* 1in) long with five to 11 alternate leaflets which are usually about 1cm ($\frac{2}{5}$in) long. The inflorescence is a many-flowered dense raceme, a pinkish-red in colour on a peduncle from 1–4cm ($\frac{2}{5}$–1$\frac{1}{2}$in) long. It is widespread throughout all districts in disturbed grassland up to 2,300m (7,500ft). Flower: *c.* 5mm (*c.* $\frac{3}{16}$in) long.

I. tanganyikensis is a stiff erect herb up to 1m (3$\frac{1}{4}$ft) tall, covered in short spreading hairs with leaves up to 5cm (2in) long with seven to 15 leaflets which are channelled and sticky at the margins. The inflorescence is two- to three-flowered, the calyx lobes are usually gland-tipped and the corolla is pale red in colour. It is found in grassland and bushland on rocky or sandy soils in Mau, Mumias, Kisii, Narok, Rift Valley, Machakos and Nairobi from 1,100–2,000m (3,500–6,600ft). Flower: corolla 7mm (*c.* $\frac{1}{4}$–$\frac{5}{16}$in) long.

Macrotyloma axillare   Plate 14 (89)
A downy climber with elliptic leaflets and yellow flowers found in evergreen forest edges and bushland at altitudes up to 2,500m (8,200ft). To visitors from Europe or America, it looks at first like a yellow Sweet Pea. Flower: *c.* 1cm ($\frac{3}{8}$in) across.

M. uniflorum is similar in appearance but has slightly smaller yellow flowers and is found in hot dry bushland in Magadi and Machakos districts at altitudes up to 1,200m (4,000ft).

Milletta dura is a shrub or tree up to 10$\frac{1}{2}$m (35ft) with ash-grey longitudinally striate bark. The leaves are imparipinnate with leaflets which are reddish and downy when young but hairless above and covered with minute short soft hairs below when mature and generally oblong to oblanceolate-oblong, 38–84mm (1$\frac{1}{2}$–3$\frac{1}{2}$in) long and 12.5–35mm ($\frac{1}{2}$–1$\frac{1}{4}$in) broad. The lilac coloured flowers, rather like those of Wisteria to visitors from overseas, are borne in clusters, three or four together on pendent panicles, 10–20cm (4–8in) long. This is a tree often seen around Mt Kenya at forest edges and in secondary scrub from 1,200–1,500m (4,000–5,000ft) in the Embu and Meru districts on the wetter side of the mountain. Flower: panicle 10–20cm (4–8in) long.

Pseudarthria hookeri   Plate 35 (221)
An erect plant with panicles of pink flowers at the leaf axils and pinnately trifoliolate leaves. It is common in wooded grassland at altitudes up to 2,290m (7,500ft). Flower: *c.* 7mm ($\frac{1}{4}$in) long.

P. confertiflora, less common than *P. hookeri*, and generally found at higher altitudes, 900–2,290m (2,950–7,500ft) in upland wooded grassland, has more crowded, spike-like pink flowers. Flower: *c.* 7mm ($\frac{1}{4}$in) long.

Rhynchosia holstii   **Plate 23** (148)
A trailing or twining plant with ovate to rhomboid leaves and long racemes of yellow flowers streaked with red (rather like widely spaced sweet pea flowers). It is found in rocky grassland, particularly around Nairobi, in Embu and Machakos, up to 2,100m (7,000ft). Flower: *c.* 15mm ($\frac{5}{8}$in) long.

Rhynchosia usambarensis   **Plate 22** (141)
A glandular and spreading, hairy, twining herb with ovate, acute leaves which have paler areas near the veins, and long pedunculate racemes of orange-yellow flowers. It is locally common in upland grassland and forest edges from 1,800–2,400m (6,000–8,000ft). Flower: *c.* 1cm ($\frac{2}{5}$in) long.

In all there are 28 different species of *Rhynchosia* in Kenya. All except *R. albissima* and *R. hirta* have yellow to orange flowers tinged or streaked with red. Their pods have only one or two seeds and their leaves are gland-dotted below, although this may be hard to detect in species which are very hairy. In addition to the two species illustrated they include:

R. albissima with yellow and purple flowers which is common at the coast but rarely found elsewhere. Flower: *c.* 12mm ($\frac{1}{2}$in) long, 8mm ($\frac{5}{16}$in) wide.

R. densiflora has yellow flowers and a low prostrate habit. It is found in stony grassland from Mumias to Machakos, from 1,000–2,100m (3,300–6,900ft). Flower: 7–14mm ($\frac{1}{4}$–$\frac{1}{2}$in) long.

R. hirta has dull white-green flowers in racemes. Its blue seeds open in the pod when ripe. It is widespread in dry woodland edges and combretum bushland, from 1–1,800m (3–5,900ft). Flower: 2cm ($\frac{3}{4}$in) long.

R. orthobotrya is a glandular-hairy woody herb with ovate leaves and long spikes of small yellow and red subsessile flowers. It is found in Baringo and westwards, in wooded grassland, from 1,000–2,100m (3,300–6,900ft). Flower: *c.* 10mm ($\frac{3}{8}$in) long.

Sesbania sesban is a shrub or small tree up to 6m (20ft) in height with hairy or downy branchlets. The leaves are up to 10cm (4in) long with leaflets up to 7.5cm (3in) long and in nine to 27 pairs in number, covered with short soft hairs. The flowers are 1.25cm ($\frac{1}{2}$in) long, yellow in colour with a plain or mottled standard. The seed pods are up to 11cm ($4\frac{3}{8}$in) long. It is widespread in most districts from 100–2,200m (300–7,200ft) but not common below 1,000m (3,280ft) and is usually found near water. Flower: *c.* 2cm ($\frac{3}{4}$in) across.

Tephrosia holstii   **Plate 25** (158)
An annual or perennial, yellowish hairy herb with unifoliolate leaves. The flowers are orange or brick red, usually in short dense terminal pseudo-racemes but also often in the axil of the uppermost leaf. The standard, upper

petal is hairy, the outside about 12mm ($\frac{1}{2}$in) long and the style is hairless and curved into a semi-circle. It is found in upland grassland and forest margins from 1,500–2,400m (5,000–8,000ft) in the Mau, Tinderet, Kitui, Mumias, Embu, Machakos and Kajiado districts and around Nairobi. Flower: standard 12mm ($\frac{1}{2}$in) long.

Tephrosia interrupta   Plate 31 (196)
A robust, bushy, woody herb with leaves formed of nine to twenty-one leaflets. Its purple flowers are grouped in darkly-haired terminal, pseudo-racemes with several flowers at each node and short lateral branches sometimes developed with the lower nodes well separated. The standard, upper petal, is covered with brown hairs. It is common in scrub margins, the edges of bush patches and on rocky outcrops at 1,575–2,800m (5,250–9,250ft), chiefly where cloud or mist is frequent. Flower: standard 14–20mm (c. $\frac{5}{8}$–$\frac{3}{4}$in) long.

Trifolium burchellianum subsp. johnstonii   Plate 42 (272)
A perennial with a tap-root, its stems, hairless (or nearly so), creeping or rooting at the nodes or, less often, ascending. Its leaflets are hairless (or nearly so), mostly cuneate-obovate, cuneate-oblong or cuneate-elliptic, emarginate or, less often, truncate or rounded at the tip. Inflorescences are many-flowered and more or less round with stout pedicels. The corolla is purple. It is found in moist upland grassland, moist forest edges and glades or moorland openings at 1,650–3,500m (5,500–11,500ft) all over Kenya but is rare in the alpine zone. The flower illustrated is seen amongst the leaves of *Alchemilla*. Flower head: 2–3cm ($\frac{3}{4}$–1$\frac{1}{8}$in) across.

Trifolium cryptopodium   Plate 43 (279)
A perennial with creeping stems which root at the nodes. It is very much dwarfed and compact at higher altitudes. There is no free leaf stalk between the stipules and the cuneate-obovate toothed leaflets. The mauve flowers are arranged in compact hemispherical heads of 20–30 blossoms. The seed pods are tiny and hidden in the calyx and bear only one or two seeds. It is common at 1,800–4,100m (5,900–13,500ft) in moist open places in the upland forest zone and in all sorts of grassy, rocky or moist localities in the moorland and alpine zones of the wetter mountains of Kenya. Flower: c. 9mm ($\frac{3}{8}$in) long.

Trifolium rueppellianum   Plate 39 (249)
An annual with hairless, erect, or sometimes prostrate stems, not rooting at the nodes. Its hairless leaflets are oval, oblong or obovate, rarely broadly lanceolate, and less than three times as long as they are wide, rounded and usually blunt ended. The inflorescence is usually 15–30 flowered and more or less round and the corolla usually purple, although on rare occasions it may be white. It is found in upland grassland, moorland tracks in forest or as a weed in cultivated land, usually in rather wet places at 1,500–2,250m

(5,000–11,000ft) in central and western Kenya. Inflorescence: *c.* 37mm (1½in) across.

Trifolium semipilosum A Kenya white clover, and a perennial with a strong taproot and prostrate stems covered in long soft hairs and which often root at the nodes. The leaflets are orbicular, elliptic, oblong-elliptic, ovate or cuneate-obovate; rounded, truncate, or emarginate at the tip but with soft silky hairs underneath though these can be few in number, at the margins, on the midribs and the two lateral leaflets beneath. These silky hairs are on one half of the leaflet only, hence the name *semipilosum*. The head-like inflorescence is white or pale pink in colour. The pedicels are reflexed in fruit which distinguishes it from most other East African clovers. Inflorescence: *c.* 2cm (¾in) across; the standard 8–9mm (*c.* $\frac{5}{16}$in) long.

Vigna sp.*   **Plate 38** (242)
At first glance the flowers of the Vigna genus remind one of sweet peas. All Vigna are climbing or trailing plants and many prefer damp or moist ground from 1–2,450m (3–8,100ft), either near or alongside swamps or forest edges. Some also grow in cultivated land, in grassland or montane grassland, and forest glades while others are found in rocky places, dry grassland, bushland and dry forest areas. The genus is fairly catholic in its habitat. The flowers range from pinkish-violet to blue-purple or an unusual shade of yellowish-green, although *V. monophylla* has yellow and mauve flowers. The illustration was photographed in the Mathews Range. Flower: *c.* 13mm (½in) across.

Vigna vexillata   **Plate 38** (243)
A perennial climber or trailer with a narrow woody rootstock. Its leaflets, down-covered on both sides, are rarely somewhat lobed with the stipules subcordate. The two- to six-flowered inflorescence is mauve and sub-umbellate, the pedicels 1–2mm ($\frac{1}{16}$in) long, the calyx with long bristly hairs which are often brownish but there are also short white hairs. It is found from 1–2,200m (3–7,200ft) in grassland, bushland and forest edges but not in dry areas and is especially widespread in central and western districts. Flower: 3cm (1⅛in) across.

V. monophylla is an erect, tufted herb from a tuberous or rhizomatous rootstock with hairless lanceolate to ovate leaves. The yellow and mauve flowers are carried on long peduncles which stand above or exceed the leaves. It is locally common in the Kitale and Western Kenya districts, from 1,000–2,100m (3,300–6,900ft). Flower: 10–14mm ($\frac{2}{5}$–½in) long.

V. schimperi is a twining plant with a large rootstock; the stems are velvety with closely pressed rust-coloured hairs which later tend to become hairless and the leaflets entire, covered in soft hairs on both sides. The inflorescence is so much condensed that it almost appears to be an umbel, with the corolla hairless and greenish yellow-orange or brown in colour, and like a rather thin half open sweet pea flower. The seed pods are carried erect, velvety in appearance with a covering of closely pressed rusty hairs and range from 4 to 9cm ($1\frac{1}{2}$–$3\frac{1}{2}$in) long. This is a widespread plant in upland grassland and forest edges from 1,500–2,300m (4,800–7,500ft) in all districts. Corolla: 18–25mm ($\frac{2}{3}$–1in) long.

34. Mimosoideae The Acacia Family

These plants are tropical or subtropical trees and shrubs or, less often, herbs with bi-pinnate or, rarely, pinnate leaves. Their flowers are small and regular, grouped in dense inflorescences. Petals are valvate in the bud and often united below to form a tube. The stamens have short anthers. There are 77 species in Kenya belonging to ten genera, more than half of them in *Acacia*.

Acacia drepanolobium   **Plate 10** (64)
Commonly known as the Whistling Thorn, this plant not only carries long and extremely spiky thorns, its branches also bear small galls like oak apples in which small ants live which sally forth to bite the lips of rhinoceros, giraffe and other browsers, providing an additional defence. Small creamy-white flowers with a mimosa-like scent seasonally cover the plant which is abundant in certain types of grassland, often on black cotton soils, such as in Nairobi National Park, at altitudes of 600–2,650m (2,000–8,700ft). Flower head: *c*. 12mm ($\frac{1}{2}$in) across.

Acacia kirkii   **Plate 32** (204)
A flat-crowned tree with a stout bole, radiating branches and greenish peeling bark and slender straight spines up to 25mm (1in) long. There are six to fourteen pairs of pinnae with a sessile gland between the lowest and between one or two of the upper – sometimes between all pairs. Leaflets are numerous, linear and pointed. The pink flowers form round heads, with peduncles solitary or clustered in the axils. It is generally found at 1,200–1,950m (4,000–6,500ft) altitudes in the Southern Province, Kiambu and Nairobi districts. Flower head: *c*. 1cm ($\frac{2}{5}$in) in diameter.

Acacia senegal   **Plate 1** (3)
A tree or bush which grows in dry bushland and usually less than 5m (16ft) high, although it will occasionally reach twice that height. It frequently forms dense thicket. The stem is short and low-branching and the crown of mature trees is flattened. Short thorns are grouped in threes at the swollen nodes, the centre one is sharply recurved, the other two more or less straight and pointing forward. The flowers, red in bud and creamy white when open, are sweetly scented and usually appear before the leaves open. The flower spikes

MIMOSOIDEAE

may be solitary or two or three together. It is found at altitudes of
120–1,680m (400–5,500ft). Flower spikes: 5–10cm (2–4in) long.

Acacia seyal   **Plate 24** (149)
A tree of the savannah growing to 9m (30ft) in height, found in colonies on
flats of black cotton soil and on stony ground at the base of hills. Its crown is
flat-topped and its stem smooth. At times new growth is covered with a
mealy, creamy-yellow or rust-red powder which comes off when rubbed to
expose the very thin bark below. The bark is shed annually, scaling off very
regularly in rectangles. On the lower part of the twigs are white thorns with
grey fleckings and red tips which are up to 6.25cm (2½in) long. They are
replaced by short recurved prickles towards the ends of the twigs. There are
two variations of this species: var. *fistula* with white bark, on which some of
the thorns are always galled with greatly swollen bases, and var. *seyal* with
red bark which rarely have galls. The yellow flowers, which appear before the
leaves open, are highly scented and borne in great profusion in round heads.
A colony when in flower is an arresting sight. The tree is widespread
throughout Kenya at altitudes of 550–1,700m (1,800–5,600ft). Each ball of
flowers: *c.* 12mm (½in) in diameter.

A. mellifera has paired, sharply recurved thorns, about 6mm (¼in) long, which
are grey with black tips. It has white spikes of flowers and is found only in the
very driest savannah. Flower spike: 25–60mm (1–2½in) long.

Albizia anthelmintica   **Plate 1** (4)
A smooth-barked, deciduous large bush or tree growing to 8m (25ft) in
height. Its leaves are bipinnate with one to four pairs of pinnae leaflets in one
to five pairs. The flowers appear before the leaves. Both calyx and corolla are
a pale green, the stamens are white. The whole gives the appearance of many
compact, tiny powder puffs grouped close together on solitary or clustered
peduncles. It is widespread in dry savannah country except in Rift Valley and
Western Kenya in the Lake area, from 80–1,500m (250–5,000ft) altitudes.
Flower head: *c.* 2cm (¾in) across.

Dichrostachys cinerea subsp. **cinerea**   **Plate 31** (198)
An acacia-like shrub or tree which grows to 5m (16ft) or occasionally as high
as 12m (40ft). Its branchlets are armed with sharp woody spines at the end of
the lateral twigs. There are two flower types. Those nearest to the point of
attachment are neuter and have ten long pink or mauve stamenoids, while
those towards the end of the branch are functional and are composed of a
pistil and ten short yellow stamens. The flowers are dense and, since they
hang down, the pink part is always above the yellow part. This subspecies is
found in coastal, southern and northern districts of Kenya at altitudes up to
1,700m (5,000ft) at forest edges, in woodland or savannah. Where over-
grazing has taken place it will form thickets. Flower: 35–75mm (1½–3in).

65

35. LORANTHACEAE

Nearly all members of this family are parasitic on trees. They depend on birds for pollination and have rather firm, often red or orange, flowers. The calyx is short, sometimes reduced to a rim, the petals are free or united and the stamens the same number as the petals and attached to them. The ovary is inferior and the fruit a berry.

There are 45 species of *Loranthus* in Kenya but modern botanical thought considers the genus too diverse and it is possible that in future it will be split up. At present six species of *Viscum* (Mistletoe) are recorded in Kenya. They were formerly in this family but are now placed in Viscaceae.

As the Loranthaceae are not pollinated by insects they need not flower after rain, when insects are on the wing. In dry areas during the dry season they, with the Aloes (also bird pollinated), may be the only plants in bloom.

Loranthus panganensis   **Plate 28** (179)
A hairless plant, with alternate, very fleshy crisped leaves. The almost stalkless flowers are pink, grey, green or dark red and have five prominent ridges below the curved lobes and stamens. This not common plant is parasitic mostly on commiphora in dry bushland at 350–1,700m (1,150–5,600ft). If the genus was divided *L. panganensis* would be placed in the *Emilianthe*. Flower: *c.* 8mm ($\frac{1}{3}$in) long.

Loranthus zizyphifolius   **Plate 43** (280)
This plant is fairly common in moister areas than *L. panganensis* and parasitic on members of the Rhus family and other evergreen shrubs. It is covered with down or short hairs, except on the flower and old leaves. Its leaves are oblanceolate and three-nerved. The flowers form almost stalkless clusters of pink or crimson with bands of green. The corolla has a bulb at the base and erect lobes; the filaments are entire. This species has been recorded in the Nairobi area and in the Aberdares, Rift Valley, Embu and Machakos districts at altitudes 1,400–2,250m (4,600–7,400ft). If the genus was divided *L. zizyphifolius* would be placed in *Tapinanthus*. Flower: *c.* 35mm (1$\frac{3}{8}$in) long.

36. VISCACEAE

The Mistletoe Family

The members of this family (formerly grouped with the Loranthaceae) are parasitic on trees.

Viscum fischeri is an hairless pendulous plant with broad or narrow oblanceolate to obovate leaves with smooth edges; the peduncle is 5–7mm (*c.*

¼in) long and bears four to seven flowers, dull greenish-yellow in colour. It is found only in Kenya from 1,600–2,300m (5,900–7,500ft). Flower: 2–4mm (*c.* ⅛in).

V. hildebrandtii *(V. schimperi)* is an hairless plant, pendulous or erect, with almost sessile (stalkless) flowers and fruit, the fruit smooth or slightly warty and the leaves reduced to scales. The flowers are yellow-green. It is found in acacia species, especially in dry country and most plants are female. It has been recorded in Mau, Mt Kenya, Mumias, Machakos and Nairobi from 600–1,800m (2,000–5,900ft). Flower: 2–4mm (*c.* ⅛in).

V. nervosum is similar to *V. fischeri* but its elliptic leaves have crisped edges and the one to three flowers are grouped together on a short peduncle. Altitude 0–2,300m (0–7,500ft). Flower: 2–4mm (*c.* ⅛in).

V. tuberculatum is the most widespread mistletoe in Kenya. The plant is hairless, erect or pendulous with usually yellowish, obovate to oblanceolate leaves. The flowers are dull greenish-yellow in colour in more or less sessile clusters. It is found in all upland dry woodland over most of upland Kenya from 1,500–2,500m (5,000–8,200ft) in altitude. Flower: 2–4mm (*c.* ⅛in).

37. VITACEAE
The Vine Family

Most of this family are plants which climb by means of tendrils but, less often, are also erect herbs, shrubs and rarely, trees. Their leaves are alternate, often with stipules simple or palmated or pinnatifid, three- to five- (or even up to seven-) foliolate. The small flowers are yellowish or reddish. The calyx is entire or toothed, the petals free valvate and the stamens opposite to the petals and of the same number. The ovary is superior and the fruit a berry. There are 28 species in Kenya belonging to five genera.

There are more than 15 recorded species of *Cyphostemma* in Kenya with a wide range of habitat, rainfall and altitude, some preferring dry or rocky bushland, others widespread in bush grassland and still others found in upland or montane forest areas.

Cyphostemma orondo   **Plate 5** (31)
A climbing, often trailing, rarely erect herb which grows from a swollen tuberous taproot with or without tendrils. It has three to seven leaflets which are linear and elliptical and densely covered with down underneath. Its pale, greenish-yellow flowers form inflorescences 22–28cm (⅞–1⅛in) across. It is common in bushed grassland at 1,200–2,250m (4,000–7,500ft) over most of Kenya. Flower: *c.* 4mm (*c.* ⅛in) across.

38.   RUTACEAE

The Orange Family

A small to medium size tropical and warm temperate family of trees, shrubs shrublets and, less often, herbs, of which only trees and shrubs are present in Kenya. Their leaves are dotted with translucent oil glands. Their flowers are usually rather small, regular, free and four to five in number. Stamens are equal in number to the petals or twice as many. Their ovaries consist of four or five more or less free carpels, with styles distinct or connate. The fruit is usually indehiscent. There are 15 species in Kenya belonging to ten genera.

Calodendrum capense   **Plate 34** (214)

A magnificent flowering tree, popularly known as the Cape Chestnut. Its flowers, carried in large terminal panicles all over the head and sides of the tree, are almost a cyclamen-lilac in colour. It has two flowering seasons: February to early May and late August to early December, and grows throughout the central forest areas of Kenya, including the Taita Hills at 1,520–2,130m (5,000–7,000ft). Flower: petals *c*. 3cm (1⅛in).

39.   SAPINDACEAE

A medium-sized family of tropical and subtropical trees, shrubs or climbers. Their alternate leaves are usually compound and without stipules. The flowers are usually small, regular and five in number with sepals and petals free. There are four to five free stamens and often eight, and the superior ovary is usually tri-locular. There are 37 species in Kenya belonging to 20 genera.

Dodonaea viscosa   **Plate 27** (170)

A shrub or tree which will usually reach a height of 2–4m (6–12ft). It has red-brown, viscous and hairless branchlets; thin, hairless and almost stalkless, oblanceolate leaves which are 5–10cm (2–4in) long and 12–24mm (½–1in) broad with the apex obtusely apiculate and the base long attenuate. Its flowers are yellow-green to deep creamy-white, grouped in short terminal panicles or subracemous. The pale reddish-brown fruit is flat, rounded to deeply emarginate and broadly two- or more-winged, including membraneous wings, and about 2cm (¾in) across (the illustration shows these characteristic fruits). The fruits are blown by the wind and Dodonaea is, therefore, a pioneer species when forest is invading grassland, and it is widespread at altitudes up to 2,740m (9,000ft). The wood makes good walking sticks and in dry regions the plant can be used as a hedge. Flower: 5mm (¼in) across. Fruit: 15mm (⅝in) across.

UMBELLIFERAE

40. U M B E L L I F E R A E (Apiaceae)
The Parsley Family

A large family of herbs or, rarely, trees found mainly in temperate zones. Their leaves are usually alternate and divided with a sheathing base. The small flowers, arranged in umbels, are nearly always white or yellow. They have a minute calyx, and five free petals inserted outside a well-developed disc. Styles are free and two in number and the ovary inferior, bi-locular, with one ovule in each loculus, and when dry splits into two halves, usually with tubes containing oil. There are 52 species in Kenya belonging to 27 genera and they are mainly found in areas above 1,000m (3,250ft).

Caucalis incognita is a weak-stemmed annual herb densely covered with short hairs (tomentose) often subscandent with three times pinnatisect leaves, ovate to deltoid in outline, with ovate to oblong dentate segments. The umbels are more or less sessile in a head and the flowers have white petals though in rare instances these can be purple. It is abundant in all upland areas in forest edges and grassland and the fruits can be a nuisance sticking to one's trousers or to one's dog. Widespread in its altitude range from 1,600–3,300m (5,900–10,800ft). Flower: The dense head-like umbel is 1–2cm ($\frac{2}{5}-\frac{3}{4}$in) across.

Haplosciadium abyssinicum   **Plate 10** (66)
A perennial rosette herb with pinnate leaves. Its white flowers spring out from the rosette of leaves and are always close to the ground. It is a plant of alpine and high grassland areas at 2,150–4,550m (7,000–13,100ft). Flower: c. 4mm ($\frac{1}{8}$in) across.

Oenanthe palustris is a creeping perennial, rooting at the nodes, robust in-growth, with three times pinnate or ternate leaves, the leaf segments are acute in outline with short bracteoles. The flowers are greenish white. It is locally common around open water and by streamsides and is recorded in Elgon, Tinderet, Mau and Aberdares from 1,800–2,700m (6,000–8,850ft). It is poisonous to stock. Flower: the umbels are compound; the main umbel c. 4cm (1½in) across composed of about 15 small umbels each c. 8mm ($\frac{5}{16}$in) across.

O. procumbens is similar to *O. palustris* but smaller and less robust and the leaf segments are triangular in outline with the leaf segments serrate. Flowers greenish white. It is a fairly common plant on the shady floor of bamboo forest from 2,100–3,200m (7,000–10,500ft).

69

41. ERICACEAE

The Heather Family

A medium-sized family of shrublets, shrubs or small trees, rare in the tropics but very well represented in South Africa and South East Asia. Their simple leaves are often small and linear, without stipules. Stamens usually number twice as many as their corolla tubes and fruit is usually in capsule form. There are nine species in Kenya belonging to four genera and all are found above 1,520m (5,000ft).

Blaeria filago   **Plate 37** (235)
A low, hairy shrub with numerous erect, unbranched stems bearing racemes of pink flowers. It is found in disturbed, often burnt, alpine moorland at 2,000–4,250m (9,500–13,950ft). Flower: 2–4mm ($\frac{1}{8}$in) long.

42. APOCYNACEAE

Periwinkle Family, Desert Rose Family, Arrow Poison Family

A large family of trees, shrubs, lianes or, rarely, herbs almost confined to the tropics and subtropics, often poisonous or producing important medicinal drugs, nearly always with a clear or milky latex which may contain rubber. Their leaves are entire, nearly always opposite, without stipules and pinnativeined. The flowers are regular, the calyx of five free or almost free sepals. The tubular corolla is five-lobed and there are five stamens, their anthers free or slightly touching. The ovary is superior and often separates into two follicles in fruit. The seeds often have tufts of long hair at one or both ends. There are 37 species in Kenya belonging to 21 genera.

Adenium obesum   **Plate 31** (200)
A widespread succulent shrub, sometimes a small tree, from 0.3–3m (1–10ft) high. Its flowers vary from pink to deep rose. They are tubular in form with petals turned out at the end of the tube and the base of the stem swollen. This is a plant of arid areas, found in rocky, sandy and low altitude districts all over Kenya from 50–1,230m (160–4,000ft). Flower: c. 5cm (2in) long; 2.5cm (1in) across.

Acokanthera schimperi *(A. friesiorum)*   **Plate 5** (35)
A heavily foliaged evergreen tree which grows to 5–7.5m (15–25ft) in height and occasionally reaches 12m (40ft) or more. Its leaves are opposite, elliptic or broadly elliptic or, sometimes, obovate, mostly 25–55mm (1–2$\frac{1}{4}$in) long and about 25mm (1in) broad, acute or obtuse at the apex, mucronate, shining above and dull beneath. The flower clusters are axillary, stalkless or nearly

so, the tubular flowers white or white flushed with pink and fragrant; the corolla 8–12mm ($\frac{1}{3}$–$\frac{1}{2}$in) wide and the berry purple black when ripe. It is found at the edges of dry forest or in evergreen bushland at 1,100–2,300m (3,600–7,500ft). A decoction from the leaves and bark produces the deadly arrow poison used by the Akamba and by poachers. Flower: corolla c. 6mm ($\frac{1}{4}$in) across; tube 8mm ($\frac{1}{8}$in) long.

Carissa edulis   **Plate 33** (211)
A scrambling bush with many branches, growing to 3m (10ft) in height, with simple or bifurcated spines. The leaves are ovate to ovate-lanceolate or elliptical and about 5cm (2in) long. The flowers are white inside and red outside and are carried in terminal corymbose racemes. It is found in most districts with a reasonable rainfall from sea level to 2,000m (6,500ft) in bush country or at forest edges. It is sometimes seen scrambling out of ant heaps and one example near the Hippo Pool in Nairobi National Park climbs to 18m (60ft) high. Flower: c. 12mm ($\frac{1}{2}$in) across.

43. ASCLEPIADACEAE

A large tropical and warm temperate family of herbs, twiners, lianes or stem-succulents, more rarely shrublets or shrubs, and never true trees, which is closely related to the *Apocynaceae*. They differ from that family in that the stamens unite to form a solid mass around the style and the pollen unites into waxy masses (pollinia) as in the *Orchidaceae*. A corona is often present inside the corolla. The united part of the corolla is often very short. Fruit consisting of two follicles (or one by abortion) contains numerous feathered, winged or flattened seeds. There are at least 120 species in Kenya belonging to 45 genera.

Calotropis procera   **Plate 42** (273)
A tall plant with soft woody stems. The leaves spring from the widely-spaced branches at intervals up the stem and are ovate and markedly veined. The closely-massed flowers are purple, violet or white. It is common in ground which has been disturbed, such as old fields, and especially where seasonally flooded in arid country. It is fairly widespread from Mumias to Kajiado at altitudes of 300–1,200m (1,000–3,900ft). Flower: 20–24mm (c. $\frac{7}{8}$in) across.

Caralluma spp. The *Caralluma* species of which 17 have been recorded in Kenya are generally found in dry, rocky or stony areas. One or two of them tolerate dry sandy alkaline soils, e g. *C. speciosa* and *C. socotrana*. They are erect or creeping fleshy plants without leaves with four to six angles on each stem though occasionally there may be only three. The flowers in most species are purple black to intense dark black in colour. Solitary or in lateral or terminal heads. Often they look like stiff dark mop heads standing up out of the fleshy succulent type stems. Many of them grow at lower altitudes from 274–1,200m (900–4,000ft) in semi arid areas in the North, North East and East of Kenya.

Caralluma foetida   **Plate 30** (193)
A massive erect succulent with 4 angled stem up to 4cm (1½in) thick with a large head like a small mop of hairy smallish black-purple or dark violet flowers. It is an uncommon plant and found in dry alluvial country, from 600–2,000m (2,000–6,600ft). Flower: 12mm (½in) across.

C. dummeri is a decumbent fleshy perennial with ascending often variegated stems bearing lines of conical projections. The greenish or cream flowers are more or less terminal, pedicillate, with or without hairs inside. It is probably the most common *asclepiad* and is to be found in combretum woodland and adjacent grassland in rocky places with a sandy soil, throughout Kenya in its altitude range, 1,200–1,650m (3,700–5,400ft).
  The flower is often five-petalled with an open throat, not like a mop head as in the species noted above. Flower: 30–40mm (1⅛–1½in) across.

C. speciosa is similar in habit to *C. foetida* but has shorter stems and fewer and much larger flowers. It is found in dry alkaline country as noted above, from 550–900m (1,800–3,000ft). Flower: 45mm (1¾in) across.

C. socotrana is an erect caespitose fleshy perennial with cylindrical or obscurely angled stems bearing terminal groups of two to three black purple flowers. It has only been recorded in alkaline alluvial soil or stony ground at Magadi. Altitude range, 850–1,200m (2,800–3,750ft). Flower: 20–30mm (¾–1¼in) across.

Ceropegia ballyana   **Plate 8** (52)
A hairless, succulent climber with broad oblong or elliptic leaves and large solitary flowers of most unusual appearance. The corolla is greenish to yellow with purple spots and long lobes ending acutely. A plant of dry bushland, it often entwines itself high up in the branches of medium sized trees and high bush, from 1,200–1,400m (3,950–4,600ft). Flower: *c.* 65mm (2½in) long.

Ceropegia succulenta   **Plate 8** (53)
A climbing or, less frequently, erect herb with a thick, succulent stem. The leaf nodules are prominent or depressed; the leaves large oval-elliptic with white veins. The flowers are on a peduncle 5–10cm (2–4in) long and have a yellow-green corolla with maroon spots and whitish lobes with green tips and short ciliate hairs on the edges. It is found in dry forest in the Aberdares, Nairobi, Narok and Rift Valley districts. The flowers appear in the treetops and thus are not often seen. Altitude range, 1,400–2,800m (4,600–9,000ft). Flower: *c.* 55mm (2¼in) long.

ASCLEPIADACEAE

Edithcolea grandis   Plate 23 (144)
A low succulent, leafless plant with quite short, half erect, half prostrate
stems which have horny, conical, yellow knobs upon them. Its very
conspicuous flowers are purple and yellow, edged with vibratile club-shaped
hairs. A rare plant, it is found in dry rocky country at 900–1,830m
(3,000–6,000ft). It is in danger of extermination and should *not* be collected.
Districts such as Nairobi are too wet and cool for this and similar succulents
which will not grow there even if transplanted. Flower: up to 12cm (4¾in)
across.

Gomphocarpus kaessneri   Plate 15 (99)
A branching bush perennial about 1m (3¼ft) tall with a milky juice and a
yellowish green corolla with a conspicuous dark chocolate corona. As in all
species of *Gomphocarpus* the fruit is inflated and conspicuous, like a small
bladder. It is locally common in grassy stony places at 900–1,830m
(3,000–6,000ft) in Rift Valley, Magadi, Machakos, Nairobi and Kajiado
districts. It is generally replaced in Western Kenya by *G. semilunatus* though
G. kaessneri has been recorded in the Mumias area. Flower: corolla *c.* 15mm
(⅝in) across.

G. fruticosus is a branched erect shrub with needle-shaped to linear-oblong
leaves and white and maroon flowers: the fruits are ovate in outline like
sharply pointed pears and covered in almost hairless purple bristles. The
leaves are usually up to 8cm (3in) in length. It is the commonest *Gomphocarpus* in Kenya and is found in dry montane grassland and along water courses
in warmer lowland country throughout Kenya in its altitude range, at
950–2,700m (3,100–8,900ft). Flower: 14mm (⅝in) across.

G. integer is a delicate erect sparsely branched perennial with white woolly
hairs on young plants and needle shaped leaves. The flowers are yellow, green
and pink and the fruits ovate-acuminate in outline with a few hairless bristles
on one side or entirely smooth. It is locally common in the Aberdares, Kisii,
Narok, Baringo, Rift Valley, Nanyuki, Machakos and Nairobi at
900–2,150m (2,950–7,050ft). Flower: *c.* 18mm (*c.* ¾in) across.

G. semilunatus is a large erect perennial with crowded lanceolate leaves and
purple-pink flower; corona mostly with an erect tooth within the central
hollow. The fruit is covered with short soft hairs (downy) more or less oval in
shape and thickly covered with slightly rough bristles and is reminiscent of a
small bladder covered in prickles. It is a common species especially in
Western Kenya and is found growing in disturbed places and on flooded
grassland or roadsides in medium altitude grasslands. Recorded in Elgon,
Tinderet, Mau, Aberdares, Kitale, Mumias, Kisii, Narok and Rift Valley,
from 1,300–2,550m (4,300–8,400ft). Flower: 16mm (⅝in) across.

73

G. stenophyllus is similar to *G. integer* but with yellowish or reddish flowers and a much narrower smooth fruit pointed at the top. It is also locally common in dry grassland or often on disturbed ground or rocky soils at medium altitudes in Elgon, Tinderet, Mau, Aberdares, Kitale, Nanyuki, Machakos, Nairobi and Kajiado, from 1,400–2,700m (4,600–8,900ft). Flower: 12mm ($\frac{1}{2}$in) across.

Stapelia semota   **Plate 22** (139)
An uncommon short stem-succulent which belongs to a large genus that is almost confined to southern Africa. Many botanists consider that the genus should be subdivided and would probably rename this *Orbea semota*. The leaves are very much reduced, being the tips of succulent spine-like processes. The flowers are usually chocolate-coloured. The yellow variety illustrated used to occur in Nairobi but is now thought to be extinct as a wild plant. Altitude range 1,500–1,800m (4,900–c. 6,000ft). Flower: c. 55mm ($2\frac{1}{4}$in) across.

RUBIACEAE

The Coffee or Madder Family

A very large family of trees, shrubs, climbers and herbs, mainly tropical but with some herbaceous genera in temperate regions. Their leaves are entire, opposite or, less often, whorled, with interpetiolar stipules. The flowers are regular with the corolla usually tubular, the stamens of the same number as the corolla lobes and the ovary inferior. There are about 270 species in Kenya belonging to 67 genera.

Carphalea glaucescens *(Dirichletia glaucescens)*   **Plate 1** (2)
An erect or scrambling shrub 60–350cm (2–10ft) tall. The corolla is tubular, white or pale pink and has four or five short spreading lobes. The pinkish-green calyx limb is asymmetric, more or less heart-shaped. It grows and persists until the fruiting stage and is usually the most conspicuous part of the flower. This plant is found in dry bushland at altitudes of 200–900m (650–3,000ft). Flower: corolla c. 2cm ($\frac{3}{4}$in) long.

Galium aparinoides is a 'sticky' climber or scrambler with oblanceolate, rounded leaves, ending abruptly in a sharp point (apiculate). The brownish-yellow flowers are arranged in lateral cymes. It is locally common on montane forest edges and recorded in the Cheranganis, Mau, Aberdares, Mt Kenya, Kitale and Kajiado from 1,700–3,700m (5,600–12,100ft). Flower: c. 4mm (c. $\frac{1}{6}$in) across.

Gardenia ternifolia var. **jovis-tonantis**   **Plate 7** (42)
A savannah shrub or tree which grows to 5m (14ft) in height, but usually

74

stunted and twisted with pale bark. The fragrant, creamy-white flowers have a pronounced corolla and their petals are sometimes slightly twisted and their lobes twisted in bud. The woody fruit is the size and shape of a chicken's egg. It is found in western Kenya, Kitale, the Cheranganis, Kajiado and Machakos districts and in coastal areas at altitudes up to 2,100m (6,900ft). It is very closely related to a number of other species, including the sweet-smelling gardenia of the florists' shops. Flower: corolla 45–100mm ($1\frac{3}{4}$–4in) across.

Gardenia volkensii   Plate 12 (75)
A small branching deciduous tree with light grey bark. Its hairless leaves are arranged in pairs from the ends of three whorled branches. Broadly spoon-shaped and emarginate with a blunt apex, they are 25mm (1in) long and broad. The flowers are white and fragrant. It is widespread in Kenya from sea level up to 1,830m (6,000ft) and is often found in bush in areas of medium rainfall. Flower: 10–11cm (c. 4in) long.

Otomeria oculata   Plate 35 (222)
A herb with many erect, unbranched stems and ovate, lanceolate leaves. The pink, or sometimes white, corolla has a dark centre, the tube is narrow and cylindrical and the spreading lobes 5 10mm ($\frac{3}{16}$ $\frac{3}{8}$in) long. It is uncommon and found in dry rocky grassland in such districts as Baringo, Nanyuki, Embu and Machakos at altitudes 530–1,650m (1,750–5,400ft). Flower: corolla 18–32mm ($\frac{3}{4}$–$1\frac{1}{4}$in) long.

O. elatior, which is much more rare, and has scarlet flowers is found in swampy places in wooded grassland in Western Kenya. Flower: corolla 17–27mm ($\frac{5}{8}$–1in) long.

Pentanisia ouranogyne   Plate 45 (288)
A rhizomatous low-growing herbaceous plant with linear to lanceolate leaves. The flowers are bright blue on terminal corymbs and, at first sight, remind one of a brilliant blue verbena. It is often seen along roadsides and in other areas of disturbed ground such as the surrounds of hut sites. It thrives in dry country, especially where a small amount of rainfall run off can augment the normal water supply. Widespread in Kenya it favours altitudes 550–2,400m (1,800–7,875ft). Flower: corolla tube c. 7mm ($\frac{1}{4}$in).

Pentas lanceolata   Plate 41 (262)
An erect branched woody shrub with ovate-lanceolate leaves and mauve to white flowers. It grows at forest edges at 1,520–3,000m (5,000–10,000ft). The flower head is usually wider, flatter and more densely packed than in our photograph with flowers on the ends of their corollas, reminiscent of those of the garden Milfoil. Flower: 3mm ($\frac{1}{8}$in) long; corolla c. 15mm ($\frac{5}{8}$in) across, corolla tube 2–4cm ($\frac{3}{4}$–$1\frac{1}{2}$in) long.

Pentas parvifolia **Plate 28** (178)
An erect shrub with elliptic lanceolate leaves and usually with dense (though sometimes loose) corymbs of bright red flowers with long thin corolla tubes. It is common in dry bushland and wooded grassland at 900–1,500m (3,000–5,000ft) and can be seen growing in the garden around Ngulia Lodge in Tsavo West, transplanted from the wild, and also in mass on the edges of the lava belts in that Park. Inflorescence: *c.* 5cm (2in) across; corolla tube: 8–14mm ($\frac{3}{8}$–$\frac{5}{8}$in) long.

P. longiflora has opposite leaves and a loose inflorescence of several separate corymbs. Locally common throughout Kenya in dry wooded grassland often with combretum from 1,000–2,400m (3,000–7,900ft). Flower: white to cream corolla tube 25–40mm (1–1$\frac{5}{8}$in) long.

P. zanzibarica is similar to *P. lanceolata* but its blue to purple-pink flowers are shorter. It is common in dry grassland, especially in the Rift Valley, but also recorded in Tinderet, Mau, Londiani, Aberdares, Kitale, Narok, Nairobi and Kajiado from 1–2,500m (3–8,200ft). Flower: corolla tube 6–9mm (*c.* $\frac{1}{4}$–$\frac{3}{8}$in) long.

45.   CAPRIFOLIACEAE

The Honeysuckle Family

A small, medium-sized family found mainly in northern temperate zones consisting of shrubs, small trees and, more rarely, of herbs. Their leaves are opposite. Ovaries are superior. *Sambucus* is the only genus in East Africa and is sometimes treated as the only genus in *Sambucaceae*. The Kenyan species is closely related to one in the Himalayas. Strangely, no species of *Sambucus* has ever been recorded in Ethiopia.

Sambucus africana **Plate 4** (25)
A fleshy herb which grows to 5m (16ft) which is allied to the Elder of European hedgerows although its closest relative grows in the Himalayas. Its leaflets are obovate, large, sharply serrate, acute, acuminate, asymmetric or irregularly adhering to the petiole and covered with very fine down. The petals of the flower are white, often a bright creamy white, the calyx minutely lobed. The fruit is black and edible. It is found at 1,830–3,140m (6,000–10,300ft) in the bamboo and montane forest zone, especially where bamboo has died. Flower: *c.* 1cm ($\frac{3}{8}$in) across.

COMPOSITAE

46. COMPOSITAE (Asteraceae)
The Daisy Family

The daisies form one of the largest families, found throughout the world. It consists mainly of herbs or shrublets but includes a few real trees, among them *Brachylaena huillensis*, found in the forests around Nairobi, the wood from which is used by the Akamba wood carvers. The flowers are small (florets) and are grouped together (hence *Compositae*) in heads surrounded by involucral bracts. These flower heads may easily be mistaken for flowers, especially when the outer florets are flattened, forming rays, the involucral bracts resembling a calyx and the rays the petals. The true calyx may be absent or reduced to scales, or turned into bristles or hairs – the 'pappus'. The corolla may be tubular or split down one side and flattened – 'ligulate'. The anthers are united into a tube, up through which the style grows, pushing out the pollen. The ovary is inferior and produces a dry, single-seeded fruit called an achene.

There are nearly 400 species of Compositae in Kenya, belonging to some 95 genera. In so large a family it helps to be able to recognise the tribes. Some of the most important of these are:

Vernonieae in which florets are all tubular, so that there are no rays, are nearly always purple and their involucral bracts are in many rows.

Heliantheae in which the leaves are opposite and the involucral bracts in several rows, have yellow flowers. Ray florets are usually present and the pappus formed of bristles.

Senecioneae which have the involucral bracts in one row with only a few very much reduced bracts outside it.

Lactuceae which have strap-shaped florets which are usually yellow or blue. A milky latex is present.

Anisoppapus africanus   **Plate 20** (129)
A perennial rhizomatous plant with ascending stems and broadly ovate crenate leaves. The yellow, star-like flowers are slightly cupped and borne at the end of long flexible stalks. It is locally common in dry upland areas at 1,520–2,139m (5,000–7,000ft). Recorded in Elgon, Mau, Kitale, Kisii, Nairobi and Kajiado districts. Flower head: *c.* 1cm (⅜in) across.

Aspilia mossambicensis   **Plate 20** (127)
A much branched woody herb or shrub with rough, elliptic-lanceolate to ovate leaves. Its yellow flower heads are solitary or grouped in loose terminal cymes. It is common all over Kenya at 5–2,130m (15–7,000ft), except in the driest areas. If not controlled by burning it grows to a large size and may scramble over neighbouring bushes. Flower head: *c.* 2cm (¾in) across.

77

A. pluriseta differs from *A. mossambicensis* only in obscure details of the inflorescence. It is less common but widespread at altitudes 1,050–2,250m (3,500–7,250ft).

Anthemis tigrensis   **Plate 8** (50)
An annual or short-lived perennial with spreading branches. Its downy, twice-pinnatisect leaves are oblong in outline with the ultimate segments white. The rays of florets are also white. It is fairly common along roadsides and in disturbed places at the upper forest limits and in the lower alpine zone from 1,750–4,200m (5,800–13,800ft) but is rather rare below 2,400m (7,900ft). Flower head: including rays *c*. 3cm (1⅛in) in diameter.

Berkheya spekeana   **Plate 20** (128)
An erect annual plant with bright yellow flowers borne singly or in loose clusters. The leaves are oblong, pinnate and spiny and white-woolly below. It is a common plant at altitudes 1,800–3,000m (6,000–10,000ft) in most districts but especially in Western Kenya. Flower head: *c*. 4cm (1½in) across.

Bidens sp. A.   **Plate 19** (122)
This species has only recently been recorded in the Kibwezi and Kajiado areas and is given a temporary identification. The illustration was photographed in Tsavo West. There are 15 species of Bidens recorded in Kenya from 900–2,130m (3,000–7,000ft). They usually have yellow flowers, though more rarely white, pink or purple. They are erect shrubs with terminal corymbose or solitary heads and with opposite, divided, lobed or simple leaves. Their most characteristic feature is the barbed bristles which appear at the top of their fruits.

B. biternata tends to take the place of *B. pilosa* in western Kenya. It is more hairy and tends to have more yellow in the flowers, but it is still the detestable Black Jack, from 5–2,300m (16–7,550ft). Flower head: 1cm (⅜in) across.

B. lineata is a near relative of *B. schimperi*. It also has solitary yellow rayed flowers and is found in the same districts. Flower head: *c*. 2cm (¾in) across.

B. pilosa is an erect annual, often branching above, with pinnate mostly trifoliolate leaves and white-rayed or rayless flowers. The common 'Black Jack' weed of gardens and the most common species of *Bidens*, it nearly always grows on poor or exhausted soils from 400–2,400m (1,300–7,900ft). Flower head: 1cm (⅜in) across.

B. schimperi is a straggling annual (though sometimes found erect) with pinnatifid leaves. It has solitary yellow rayed flowers and is often found in the Nairobi, Machakos, Magadi and Kajiado districts, from 300–2,400m (1,000–7,900ft). Flower head: 3–4cm (1⅛–1½in) across.

COMPOSITAE

Bothriocline tomentosa *(Erlangea tomentosa)*   **Plate 34** (219)
An erect shrub with lanceolate-elliptic serrate leaves and terminal corymbs of violet-coloured heads. It is common on the edges of forest over most of Kenya from Kisii and Mumias in the west to Kajiado and Nyambeni in the east in the altitude range 1,300–3,000m (4,250–9,850ft), although seldom found above 2,440m (8,000ft). Flower head: *c.* 6mm (¼in) across.

B. fusca is very similar to *B. tomentosa* but has rather more purple flowers. It is common on roadsides and in disturbed places in the higher forest zones, almost always above 2,590m (8,500ft). Flower head: *c.* 5mm (*c.* ¼in) across.

Carduus keniensis   **Plate 33** (208, 209)
A spiny rosette plant with large pinnate oblong leaves which grows to a height of 1m (3ft). The flowers are borne on a single central stem as a spiny apical panicle, pinkish in colour. This is a conspicuous plant in tussocky grassland in the moorland areas of Elgon, the Aberdares, and Mt Kenya at 3,050–4,050m (10,000–13,300ft). This and the two following species belong to the same genus as the thistles common in Europe. Inflorescence: *c.* 10cm (4in) across.

C. chamaecephalus is a prostrate spiny rosette plant with thick fleshy roots and pinnatifid leaves which are tightly pressed to the ground. Purple flower heads appear in the centre of the rosette. It is common in short alpine and subalpine grassland at 3,050–3,500m (10,000–11,500ft). Flower head: *c.* 3cm (⅛in) across.

C. millefolius is very similar to *C. keniensis* but has much narrower linear leaves. The spines are shorter and finer than in *C. keniensis* and purplish in colour. It is also found in similar districts and habitats but usually in wet soil by streamsides. Each flower: *c.* 12mm (*c.* ½in) across. Each flower head: *c.* 50mm (2in) across.

Cineraria grandiflora   **Plate 19** (119)
A down-covered, erect or sometimes supported herb with a terminal corymb of rayed, yellow flower heads. Its triangular serrate leaves are petiolate, auriculate and suborbicular. It is common on roadsides, forest edges, damp cliffs and bluffs all over Kenya at altitudes of 2,000–3,350m (6,500–11,000ft). It shows considerable variation in the size of the flower head and achene according to altitude: in general, at higher altitudes the head is larger with broader and blacker achenes. Flower head: 15mm (*c.* ⅝in) across.

Cirsium vulgare   **Plate 37** (237)
An erect, often robust, annual with stalkless, oblong to elliptical, deeply pinnatifid leaves. Its large solitary purple heads have spreading bracts. It is a weed in arable land, especially in wheatfields, and is not a true native but was

COMPOSITAE

introduced from Europe. It is found at altitudes of 1,830–2,440m (6,000–8,000ft). Flower head: *c.* 3cm (1⅛in) across.

Crassocephalum mannii   **Plate 13** (86)
A much-branched, soft wooded shrub or tree which grows to 7.6m (25ft) high. Its stem is green throughout its length and its leaves are serrate, oblong-elliptic, up to 10cm (4in) wide and 45cm (18in) long with the apex acuminate and the base cuneate. The small, yellow, unpleasantly-scented flowers are all of one kind forming a head of dense panicled cymes, in a terminal inflorescence. It is widespread throughout Kenya in scrub in wetter areas at altitudes 1,220–2,440m (4,000–8,000ft) and is often used to demarcate small holdings and even to support banana trees which are heavy with fruit. Inflorescence: up to 60cm (2ft) long.

Crassocephalum montuosum   **Plate 12** (79)
An erect, woody annual or weak perennial with ovate to elliptic, simple to basally pinnatifid, hairless leaves. The flowers are in tight terminal clusters of pale yellow heads. It is common in clearings in montane forest over most of Kenya at altitudes of 2,130–2,900m (7,000–9,500ft). Flower head: *c.* 6mm (*c.* ¼in) across.

C. bojeri is a widespread, hairless, thinly succulent climber with deeply pinnatifid, oblong leaves and terminal panicles of yellow flower heads in crowded umbels. It is common in all upland forest and woodland edges. Flower head: *c.* 7mm (*c.* ¼in) across.

Crassocephalum vitellinum   **Plate 20** (126)
A trailing perennial herb with ovate, often auriculate leaves and solitary long pedunculate, orange-yellow flower heads. It is common in grassy clearings in upland forest and woodland throughout Kenya at altitudes 1,070–2,500m (3,500–8,200ft). Flower head: *c.* 11mm (*c.* ½in) across.

Echinops amplexicaulis   **Plate 27** (173)
A robust erect herb with usually stalkless leaves which are shallowly lobed and ovate-elliptical. Its red florets are arranged in coarse spherical inflorescences. It is common and conspicuous in wooded grassland and at the edges of cultivation in north-western Kenya and parts of the eastern wall of the Rift Valley at 1,700–2,400m (5,600–7,900ft). It is recorded in Elgon, Cheranganis, Mau, Aberdares, Tinderet, Kitale, Mumias, Baringo and Rift Valley districts, and, in high rainfall grassland is found, on rare occasions, at altitudes down to 1,400m (4,600ft). Flower head: *c.* 6cm (2⅜in) across.

Echinops angustilobus   **Plate 3** (20)
A robust erect herb with petiolate, much pinnatifid leaves and a few medium to large, round inflorescences with whitish-grey florets. It is found in

1. *Barleria acanthoides* p. 103

2. *Carphalea glaucescens* p. 74

3. *Acacia senegal* p. 64

4. *Albizia anthelmintica* p. 65

5. *Becium obovatum* p. 116

6. *Becium* sp. A p. 110

Plate 1

7. *Chlorophytum* sp.* pp. 117–18

8. *Gladiolus ukambanensis* p. 123

9. *Bonatea steudneri* p. 125

10. *Chascanum hildebrandtii* p. 108

11. *Ethulia* sp. A p. 81

12. *Cenchrus ciliaris* p. 128

13. *Cyathula cylindrica* p. 35

Plate 2

14. *Chlorophytum tenuifolium* p. 17

15. *Clerodendrum rotundifolium* p. 108

16. *Cordia africana* p. 92

17. *Gynandropsis gynandra* p. 29

18. *Ehretia cymosa* p. 93

19. *Leucas urticifolia* p. 111

20. *Echinops angustilobus* p. 80

21. *Ornithogalum donaldsonii* p. 119

Plate 3

22. *Salvia coccinea* L. var *lactea* p. 112

23. *Rangaeris amaniensis* p. 126

24. *Phaulopsis imbricata* p. 106

25. *Sambucus africana* p. 76

26. *Swertia usambarensis* p. 89

27. *Senecio syringifolius* p. 86

28. *Streptocarpus exsertus* p. 102

29. *Tarchonanthus camphoratus* p. 87

Plate 4

30. *Heliotropium steudneri* p. 93

31. *Cyphostemma orondo* p. 67

32. *Thunbergia guerkeana* p. 107

33. *Datura stramonium* p. 94

34. *Grewia tenax* p. 46

35. *Acokanthera schimperi* p. 70

Plate 5

36. *Diaphananthe* sp.* p. 125

37. *Heliotropium undulatifolium* p. 93

38. *Hebenstretia dentata* p. 100

39. *Helichrysum glumaceum* p. 83

40. *Phytolacca dodecandra* p. 34

41. *Capparis cartilaginea* p. 28

Plate 6

42. *Gardenia ternifolia* var *jovis-tonantis* p. 74

43. *Gnidia subcordata* p. 40

44. *Plumbago zeylanica* p. 90

45. *Leucas grandis* p. 111

46. *Helichrysum brownei* p. 83

47. *Clematis brachiata* p. 26

Plate 7

48. *Nymphaea lotus* p. 27   **49.** *Oncoba routledgei* p. 41

50. *Anthemis tigrensis* p. 78   **51.** *Maerua kirkii* p. 29

52. *Ceropegia ballyana*   **53.** *Ceropegia succulenta* p. 72   **54.** *Lippia javanica* p. 109
p. 72

Plate 8

55. *Hibiscus fuscus* p. 49

56. *Hibiscus flavifolius* p. 49

57. *Protea kilimandscharica* p. 41

58. *Dombeya rotundifolia* p. 47

59. *Hibiscus vitifolius* p. 50

60. *Combretum aculeatum* p. 44

Plate 9

61. *Caucanthus albidus* p. 51

62. *Terminalia prunioides* p. 44

63. *Barleria eranthemoides* p. 103

64. *Acacia drepanolobium* p. 64

65. *Haplosciadium abyssinicum* p. 69

66. *Polystachya transvaalensis* p. 127

67. *Cyathula polycephala* p. 85

Plate 10

68. *Crassula alba* p. 30

69. *Helichrysun nandense* p. 84

70. *Maerua edulis* p. 29

71. *Maerua subcordata* p. 29

72. *Gomphrena celosioides* p. 36

73. *Senecio jolmstonii* subsp. *battiscombei* p. 85

Plate 11

74. *Gardenia volkensii* p. 75

75. *Cistanche tubulosa* p. 101

76. *Bauhinia taitensis* p. 54

77. *Crotalaria cleomifolia* p. 57

78. *Guizotia scabra* p. 82

79. *Crassocephalum montuosum* p. 80

80. *Justicia flava* p. 106

Plate 12

81. *Hibiscus ludwigii* p. 50

82. *Cassia singueana* p. 55

83. *Crotalaria mauensis* p. 58

84. *Eriosema psoraleoides* p. 58

85. *Bulbine abyssinica* p. 117

86. *Crassocephalum mannii* p. 80

87. *Ipomoea obscura* p. 98

Plate 13

88. *Nicotiana glauca* p. 94

89. *Macrotyloma axillare* p. 60

90. *Peponium vogelii* p. 42

91. *Pavonia zeylonica* p. 51

92. *Monsonia ovata* p. 37

93. *Ochna insculpta* p. 43

Plate 14

94. *Encephalartos tegulaneus* p. 25

95. *Crotalaria agatiflora* p. 56

96. *Alchemilla fischeri* p. 53

97. *Spilanthes mauritiana* p. 87

98. *Kalanchoe densiflora* p. 30

99. *Gomphocarpus kaessneri* p. 73

Plate 15

100. *Abutilon mauritianum* p. 48   **101.** *Cassia abbreviata* p. 54

102. *Helichrysum cymosum* subsp. *fruticosum* p. 83   **103.** *Psiadia punctulata (P. arabica)* p. 85

104. *Portulaca kermesina* p. 32   **105.** *Hibiscus lunariifolius* p. 50

Plate 16

106. *Ochna ovata* p. 43

107. *Pavonia patens* p. 50

108. *Taraxacum officinale* p. 87

109. *Tithonia diversifolia* p. 88

110. *Triumfetta flavescens* p. 46

111. *Senecio brassica* subsp. *brassica* p. 85

Plate 17

112. *Crotalaria laburnifolia* p. 57   **113.** *Triumfetta macrophylla* p. 47

114. *Ranunculus multifidus* p. 26   **115.** *Helichrysum odoratissimum* p. 84

116. *Verbascum sinaiticum* p. 101   **117.** *Tylosema fassoglense* p. 55   **118.** *Tagetes minuta* p. 87

Plate 18

119. *Cineraria grandiflora* p. 79

120. *Crotalaria lebrunii* p. 57

121. *Cucumis* sp.* p. 42

122. *Bidens* sp.* p. 78

123. *Tribulus cistoides* p. 36

124. *Argemone mexicana* p. 28

Plate 19

125. *Euryops brownei* p. 81

126. *Crassocephalum vitellinum* p. 80

127. *Aspilia mossambicensis* p. 77

128. *Berkheya spekeana* p. 78

129. *Anisopappus africanus* p. 77

130. *Cassia didymobotrya* p. 54

Plate 20

131. *Haplocarpha rueppellii* p. 83

132. *Gynura miniata* p. 82

133. *Hypoxis obtusa* p. 124

134. *Hibiscus aethiopicus* p. 49

135. *Hypericum revolutum* p. 45

136. *Sedum ruwenzoriense* * p. 31

Plate 21

137. *Ansellia gigantea* var. *nilotica* p. 124

138. *Eulophia stenophylla* p. 126

139. *Stapelia semota* p. 74

140. *Merremia* sp.* p. 98

141. *Rhynchosia usambarensis* p. 61

142. *Cassia grantii* p. 55

Plate 22

143. *Crotalaria axillaris* p. 57

144. *Edithcolea grandis* p. 73

145. *Hibiscus calyphyllus* p. 49

146. *Abutilon hirtum* p. 48

147. *Hypericum annulatum* p. 45

148. *Rhynchosia holstii* p. 61

Plate 23

149. *Acacia seyal* p. 65   **150.** *Delonix elata* p. 55

151. *Thunbergia alata* p. 107   **152.** *Opuntia vulgaris* p. 43

153. *Leonotis mollissima* p. 111   **154.** *Leonotis nepetifolia* p. 111

Plate 24

155. *Kalanchoe lanceolata* p. 31

156. *Kalanchoe glaucescens* p. 31

157. *Gladiolus natalensis* p. 123

158. *Tephrosia holstii* p. 61

159. *Thunbergia gregorii* p. 107

160. *Euphorbia graciliramea* p. 52

Plate 25

161. *Combretum mossambicense* p. 44

162. *Erythrina abyssinica* p. 59

163. *Aloe rabaiensis* p. 116

164. *Ruttya fruticosa* p. 107

165. *Combretum paniculatum* p. 44

166. *Euphorbia kibwezensis* p. 52

167. *Rumex usambarensis* p. 34

Plate 26

168. *Canarina abyssinica*
p. 90

169. Fruit of *C. abyssinica*
p. 90

170. *Dondonaea viscosa*
p. 68

171. *Echinops amplexicaulis* p. 117

172. *Aloe secundiflora* p. 117

173. *Aloe volkensii* p. 80

174. *Crossandra nilotica* p. 104

175. *Aloe graminicola* p. 116

Plate 27

176. *Ipomoea hederifolia* p. 96   **177.** *Cyrtanthus sanguineus* subsp. *ballyi* p. 121

178. *Pentas parvifolia* p. 76   **179.** *Loranthus panganensis* p. 66

180. *Hibiscus aponeurus* p. 49   **181.** *Impatiens niamniamensis* p. 39

Plate 28

182. *Scadoxus multiflorus* p. 122

183. *Gladiolus watsonioides* p. 123

184. *Grewia villosa* p. 46

185. *Gloriosa superba* p. 119

186. *Hydnora abyssinica* p. 27

187. *Notonia abyssinica* p. 85

188 *Salvia coccinea* var. *coccinea* p. 113

Plate 29

189. *Kigelia africana* p. 102

190. *Crassula* sp. B p. 30

191. *Achyrospermum carvalhi* p. 110

192. *Boöphone disticha* p. 121

193. *Caralluma foetida* p. 72

194. *Hagenia abyssinica* p. 53

Plate 30

195. *Ethulia scheffleri* p. 81

196. *Tephrosia interrupta* p. 62

197. *Lantana camara* p. 109

198. *Dichrostachys cinerea* subsp. *cinerea* p. 65

199. *Cycnium tubulosum* subsp. *montanum* p. 100

200. *Adenium obesum* p. 70

Plate 31

201. *Cyanotis barbata* p. 115

202. *Crossandra subacaulis* p. 104

203. *Dyschoriste* sp.* p. 105

204. *Acacia kirkii* p. 64

p.205 *Acalypha volkensii* p. 52

206. *Pseudosopubia hildebrandtii* p. 100

207. *Satureia biflora* p. 113

Plate 32

208. *Carduus keniensis* p. 79

209. *C. keniensis* (detail) p. 79

210. *Crinum macowanii* p. 121

211. *Carissa edulis* p. 71

212. *Rubus steudneri* p. 53

213. *Crassula pentandra* var. *phyturus* p. 30

Plate 33

214. *Calodendrum capense* p. 68

215. *Anagallis serpens* p. 89

216. *Grewia similis* p. 46

217. *Grewia lilacina* p. 46

218. *Oxalis obliquifolia* p. 38

219. *Bothriocline tomentosa* p. 79

Plate 34

220. *Pavonia urens* p. 51

221. *Pseudarthria hookeri* p. 60

222. *Otomeria oculata* p. 75

223. *Ammocharis tinneana* p. 120

224. *Geniosporum rotundifolium* p. 110

225. *Vernonia* sp.* p. 88

Plate 35

226. *Sphaeranthus napierae* p. 86   **227.** *Sphaeranthus cyathuloides* p. 86

228. *Hibiscus cannabinus* p. 49   **229.** *Satureia pseudosimensis* p. 113   **230.** *Ethulia* sp. A p. 81

231. *Delosperma oehleri* p. 32   **232.** *Cycnium cameronianum* p. 99

Plate 36

233. *Sphaeranthus suaveolens* * p. 87   **234.** *Digera muricata* p. 35

235. *Blaeria filago* p. 70   **236.** *Hoehnelia vernonioides*   **237.** *Cirsium vulgare* p. 79
p. 84

238. *Ipomoea cicatricosa* p. 96   **239.** *Verbena bonariensis* p. 109

Plate 37

240. *Romulea fischeri* p. 123

241. *Ghikaea speciosa* p. 100

242. *Vigna* sp.* p. 63

243. *Vigna vexillata* p. 63

244. *Gutenbergia cordifolia*
p. 82

245. *Eulophia horsfallii* p. 126

246. *Justicia* sp.* p. 106

Plate 38

247. *Senecio roseiflorus* p. 86

248. *Commicarpus pedunculosus* p. 40

249. *Trifolium rueppellianum* p. 62

250. *Gutenbergia fischeri* p. 82

251. *Lobelia holstii* p. 91

252. *Erythrochlamys spectabilis* p. 110

Plate 39

253. *Trachyandra saltii*
p. 120

254. *Cyphia glandulifera*
p. 91

255. *Anthericopsis sepalosa*
p. 114

256. *Barleria submollis* p. 104

257. *Ipomoea mombassana* p. 97

258. *Ipomoea cairica* p. 96

259. *Ipomoea hildebrandtii* subsp.
hildebrandtii p. 97

Plate 40

260. *Hypoestes verticillaris* p. 105

261. *Ipomoea spathulata* p. 98

262. *Pentas lanceolata* p. 75

263. *Justicia diclipteroides* p. 106

264. *Brillantaisia nitens* p. 104

265. *Pelargonium whytei* p. 38

266. *Geranium ocellatum* p. 37

Plate 41

267. *Abutilon longicuspe* p. 48

268. *Plectranthus cylindraceus* p. 12

269. *Scilla kirkii* p. 120

270. *Nepeta azurea* p. 112

271. *Ipomoea jaegeri* p. 97

272. *Trifolium burchellianum* subsp. *johnstonii* p. 62

273. *Calotropis procera* p. 71

Plate 42

274. *Murdannia simplex* p. 115

275. *Talinum portulacifolium* p. 32

276. *Cleome allamannii* p. 28

277. *Solanum sessilistellatum* p. 94

278. *Centemopsis kirkii* p. 35

279. *Trifolium cryptopodium* p. 62

280. *Loranthus zizyphifolius* p. 66

Plate 43

281. *Plectranthus sylvestris* p. 112

282. *Solanum* sp. Chalbi Desert p. 95

283. *Vernonia auriculifera* p. 88

284. *Solanum incanum* p. 94

285. *Clerodendrum myricoides* p. 108

286. *Vernonia galamensis* p. 88

287. *Impatiens sodenii* p. 39

Plate 44

288. *Pentanisia ouranogyne* p. 75

289. *Thunbergia holstii* p. 107

290. *Craterostigma plantagineum* p. 99

291. *Craterostigma* sp. p. 99

292. *Echiochilon lithospermoides* p. 93

293. *Salvia merjamie* p. 113

Plate 45

294. *Cynoglossum lancifolium* p. 92

295. *Barleria spinisepala* p. 104

296. *Wahlenbergia abyssinica* p. 91

297. *Cynoglossum* sp.* pp. 92–3

298. *Blepharis linariifolia* p. 104

299. *Clitoria ternatea* p. 56

300. *Commelina forskalei* p. 114

Plate 46

301. *Plectranthus barbatus* p. 112

302. *Ceratostigma abyssinicum* p. 90

303. *Acanthus eminens* p. 103

304. *Veronica abyssinica* p. 101

305. *Nymphaea caerulea* p. 27

306. *Ecbolium revolutum* p. 105

307. *Commelina* sp. A p. 114

Plate 47

308. *Lobelia keniensis* p. 91

309. *Felicia muricata* p. 81

310. *Delphinium macrocentron* p. 26

311. *Lobelia telekii* p. 91

Plate 48

grassland in high altitude zones 2,010–2,850m (6,600–9,350ft). Flower head: *c*. 5cm (2in) across.

E. hispidus is similar to *E. angustilobus* but has stiff bristles on stem and upper leaves with larger, round, grey-white inflorescences. It is locally common in upland grassland at slightly lower altitudes, 1,200–2,200m (3,900–7,200ft) in western Kenya, Narok and Rift Valley districts. Flower head: *c*. 9cm (3½in) across.

Ethulia sp. A   Plate 2 (11), 36 (230)
An erect, woody herb, generally an annual, pubescent or tomentose, with oblanceolate, linear, serrate leaves and linear phyllaries to the crowded heads. The inner achenes are often two-winged. This is a plant which grows in the central districts of Kenya: the Aberdares, Rift Valley, Machakos, Kajiado-and Nairobi. Near Nairobi, it is often found in swamp grassland. The inflorescences are corymbs of purple heads with the bracts in several rows and the florets tubular. Altitude range 1,500–2,400m (5,000–8,000ft). Flower head: *c*. 5mm (*c*. ¼in) across.

Ethulia scheffleri   Plate 31 (195)
An erect, woody, hair-covered herb with oblanceolate, linear, serrate leaves which is generally an annual. The inflorescences are corymbs of purple heads made up of tubular florets with blunt bracts in several rows. The achenes are three- to four-winged. It is found at 1,600–2,200m (5,200–7,250ft) in Narok and the Rift Valley and is common in swampy grasslands near Nairobi. Flower head: *c*. 5mm ($\frac{3}{16}$in) across.

Euryops brownei   Plate 20 (125)
An erect shrub with many branches and short leaves with dense masses of yellow, star-like flowers at the apices of the branches. It is common at the upper limits of forest areas and in lower moorland heath zones on the drier sides of the Aberdares and Mt Kenya at altitudes above 2,600m (8,500ft). Flower head: *c*. 18mm (¾in) across.

E. elgonensis is similar to *E. brownei* but with wider leaves. It is confined to Mt Elgon. Flower: 2cm (¾in) across.

E. jacksonii is a low trailing species or an erect shrub with yellow heads, similar to *E. brownei*, which is found in rocky places in dry upland areas, especially in the Rift Valley and western Aberdares. Flower: 17mm (*c*. ⅝in) across.

Felicia muricata   Plate 48 (309)
A low, erect or trailing, weakly-woody shrub, sometimes rhizomatous, which has linear leaves. It has solitary heads of spreading blue rays with a yellow

centre, the rays frequently of a deeper blue than those illustrated. It is found in dry grassland on clay soils at 1,600–2,800m (5,250–9,200ft) in Mau, Aberdares, Narok and Nairobi districts and is common in the Rift Valley. Flower head: *c*. 75mm (3in) across.

F. abyssinica subsp. **neghellensis** is closely related to *F. muricata* and also widespread in the highlands of Kenya. The two species are difficult to distinguish from each other. Flower: *c*. 75mm (3in) across.

Guizotia scabra   **Plate 12** (78)
An erect, usually rough herb with a wiry, perennial rootstalk which bears oblong, dentate or entire leaves. Its many yellow heads form a loose terminal corymb. It sometimes grows as an annual. It is common in upland grassland, especially around Nairobi, but is widespread in Kenya at altitudes 1,520–2,780m (5,000–9,000ft). Flower head: *c*. 30mm ($1\frac{1}{4}$in) across.

Gutenbergia cordifolia   **Plate 38** (244)
A small to medium, erect herb with opposite or alternate, simple leaves, usually with white hairs below. The flower heads are solitary or in terminal corymbs with purple flowerets which are tubular and bisexual. It is found in rocky, eroded or poor grassland over most of Kenya, except in the north west, at 1,200–2,400m (3,900–8,000ft). Flower head: *c*. 14mm (*c*. $\frac{5}{8}$in) across.

Gutenbergia fischeri   **Plate 39** (250)
A small, erect herb, normally perennial, with undulate leaves, white and felty below. Its purple heads form small terminal corymbs. It is found in rocky eroded grassland south of a line from Mt Kenya to Tinderet at altitudes 1,200–2,200m (4,000–7,200ft). Flower head: *c*. 6mm ($\frac{1}{4}$in) across.

G. ruepellii is similar to *G. fischeri*, except that the leaves are oblong-linear and sessile and the involucres smaller. It is found at the same altitudes north of the line from Mt Kenya to Tinderet. Flower head: 4–5mm (*c*. $\frac{3}{16}$in) across.

Gynura miniata   **Plate 21** (132)
An erect, perennial herb with oblanceolate, pinnatifid leaves. Three to seven orange-yellow flower heads are carried on a terminal corymb. All the species in this genus have yellow to orange flowers of a similar type. It is locally common in grassland on black cotton soil in the Nairobi and Kajiado districts. Flower head: *c*. 15mm ($\frac{5}{8}$in) across.

G. amplexicaulis grows erect from a creeping rootstalk. It has oblanceolate leaves and bears a few orange flower heads on a long terminal corymb. It is locally common in disturbed ground in western Kenya, Elgon, Kitale and Kisii. Flower: 12mm (*c*. $\frac{1}{2}$in) across.

COMPOSITAE

G. scandens is a weak climber or scrambler with auriculate, ovate, fleshy, serrated leaves. Its orange-yellow flowers are grouped more closely on the terminal corymb than in the two preceding species. It is found in the wetter situations of normally drier areas at altitudes up to 2,100m (7,000ft) in the Elgon, Tinderet, Mau, Aberdares, Mt Kenya, Kitale, Narok and Rift Valley districts. Flower: 11mm ($\frac{3}{8}$in) across.

G. valeriana is a weak, juicy herb with oblanceolate, pinnatifid leaves and a loose terminal corymb of yellow-orange flowers. So far it has been found only on the Chyulu Hills in the wetter forest areas. Flower: 7mm ($\frac{1}{4}$in) across.

Haplocarpha rueppellii   Plate 21 (131)
An alpine plant with generally glossy leaves, although in western Kenya they may be dull in appearance. Its flowers are a rich yellow. It grows in areas subject to frost where the soil is loose and unstable at altitudes 2,400–4,000m (7,800–13,000ft). Flower head: c. 2–3cm ($\frac{3}{4}$–$1\frac{1}{4}$in) across.

H. schimperi is a flat, rosette-leaved plant with the leaves close to the ground and small, pale yellow flowers in the centre of the rosette. It is uncommon but found in short grassy clearings in dryer mountain forest areas at 2,440–3,040m (8,000–10,000ft). Flower head: 9mm (c. $\frac{3}{8}$in) across.

Helichrysum brownei   Plate 7 (46)
A low, bushy shrub with short, linear leaves with solitary white flower heads or clustered small heads at the stem apex. The plant itself is grey-silver in colour. It is locally common in high altitude, shrubby vegetation above the heath zone on the Aberdares, and Mt Kenya above 3,350m (11,000ft). Flower head: c. 16mm ($\frac{5}{8}$in) across.

Helichrysum cymosum subsp. fruticosum   Plate 16 (102)
One of the so-called 'everlasting flowers', this is a weak or wiry, straggling plant, although it can also be low and erect with yellowish, woolly, linear, oblong or lanceolate leaves, erect or reflexed in some cases. The yellowish-brown flower heads form dense terminal balls or corymbs, 12–18mm ($\frac{1}{2}$–$\frac{3}{4}$in) across. It is a very variable plant found in a wide range of habitats in stony grassland at 1,200–4,700m (3,600–15,000ft). Flower head: c. 3mm ($\frac{1}{8}$in) across.

Helichrysum glumaceum   Plate 6 (39)
A shrubby, low-growing, grey, hairy perennial with linear acute leaves. The white or pink flowers form tight clusters in the form of racemes on naked peduncles. It is common in dry grassland and wooded grassland over most of east and central Kenya at altitudes up to 2,250m (7,400ft) and in northern areas. Flower head: c. 2mm ($\frac{1}{8}$in) across, 5mm ($\frac{1}{4}$in) long.

COMPOSITAE

H. kilimanjari is a small, wiry, erect annual with oblanceolate or oblinear, pale-backed leaves and reddish stems. The yellow to brownish-yellow flower heads are carried in a terminal corymb. An uncommon species, it is found in disturbed, burnt places at the lower end of the alpine zone on Mt Elgon, Mt Kenya, the Cheranganis and the Aberdares at 1,200–3,950m (4,000–13,000ft). Flower head: *c.* 8mm (*c.* ¼in) across.

Helichrysum nandense   Plate 11 (69)
A large, loose shrub growing to 2.7m (9ft) in height. Its white flower heads may be tinged with pink. It is generally found in the lower alpine areas, on the edges of forest areas and along roadside banks but is common from 2,100–3,000m (6,900–9,800ft). Flower head: *c.* 15mm (⅝in) across.

H. formossissum is a similar shrub to *H. nandense* but grows up to 3m (10ft) in height. Its dense corymbs of flowers are usually white, but sometimes pink. It is common and found in open, tussocky and burnt grassland and along roadsides in the bamboo zone at 2,700–4,100m (8,850–13,500ft).

Helichrysum odoratissimum   Plate 18 (115)
A rather straggling plant covered with silvery hairs, its leaves incline downwards and are linear-lanceolate. Despite its generally weak habit it has reasonably strong, erect, smooth or naked stems which support dense corymbs of yellow flower heads which have an aromatic smell. It is very common throughout Kenya, except in the driest localities, at altitudes of 910–2,100m (3,000–7,000ft) and occasionally found at lower altitudes down to 760m (2,500ft). Flower head: *c.* 6mm (¼in) long.

Hoehnelia vernonioides   Plate 37 (236)
An erect, weak, hairless and sparsely-branched shrub with oblong to narrow-elliptic, serrate leaves. The inflorescence is a terminal corymb of purple heads. It is locally abundant at 1,650–2,750m (5,350–9,000ft). Flower head: *c.* 1cm (⅜in) across.

Lactuca capensis is an erect herb usually branched only above with pinnatifid entire leaves and a diffuse mass of terminal blue flower heads. It is common everywhere in disturbed ground in the medium altitude grasslands especially along roadsides and widespread throughout Kenya. Flower: 16mm (⅝in) across.

L. glandulifera is a scrambling downy herb with pinnate or pinnatifid leaves with three to five pinnae, the lowermost with a narrowed leaf stalk. The ligules (strap-like shaped florets) are yellow inside and dull purple outside. The flower heads themselves are plum-purple when closed and yellow when open. It is locally common in the montane rain forest on Mt Elgon, the Cheranganis, Tinderet, Mau, the Aberdares, Mt Kenya and the Nyambeni Hills from 1,900–2,400m (6,200–7,900ft). Flower head: *c.* 1cm (⅖in) long.

84

Notonia abyssinica   **Plate 29** (187)
A hairless herb with ascending stems and oblanceolate to obovate leaves
which are usually entire, acute and fleshy. One to seven bright red flower
heads form loose terminal cymes. It is found in rocky soils and along bushed
stream banks at 760–2,440m (2,500–8,000ft) in western areas of Kenya.
Flower head: *c*. 15mm ($\frac{5}{8}$in) across.

N. hildebrandtii is slightly smaller than *N. abyssinica*. Carrying the same red
flower heads, it is found in rocky soils and along bushed stream banks at the
same height throughout eastern, northern and central Kenya and especially
around Nairobi. Further study may reveal that the two species are actually
only geographical races of the same plant. Flower head: *c*. 2cm ($\frac{3}{4}$in) across.

Psiadia punctulata *(P. arabica)*   **Plate 16** (103)
An erect, round-topped shrub with entire, lanceolate-elliptic, glossy leaves
which produce a gum-like secretion when young. The bright yellow flower
heads form terminal racemes. An abundant plant on the edges of disturbed
bushland, in evergreen woodland and in dry forest areas, it is found from the
Nairobi area westwards at 1,200–2,300m (4,000–7,500ft). Flower head: *c*.
5mm (*c*. $\frac{1}{4}$in) across.

Dendrosenecio

The Dendrosenecios or Giant Groundsels are either trees or shrubs growing
up to 9m (30ft) in height. Their stems are branched, ending in a rosette or
cabbage of large leaves which often hang on after dying. The dwarf species
have a sparse and flattened branching system. The taller species have deeply
furrowed corky bark; almost all species have magnificent panicles of yellow
flowers. There are now considered to be only three species of the sub-genus in
Kenya, each with its own subspecies and distribution.

Senecio brassica subsp. **brassica**   **Plate 17** (111)
A dwarf form belonging to the giant groundsel family which reaches a height
of 1.8m (6ft) when its yellow flowers are in bloom. It is confined to open
moorland at altitudes from 3,300–3,900m (10,800–12,750ft). Infloresscence:
up to 2m ($6\frac{1}{2}$ft) tall.

S. brassica subsp. **brassiciformis** is found only in the Aberdares at 3,000–
3,500m (9,850–11,500ft). Inflorescence: up to 2m ($6\frac{1}{2}$ft) tall.

Senecio johnstonii subsp. **battiscombei**   **Plate 11** (73)
A tree growing to 6m (20ft) high with ovate-lanceolate leaves which are up to
45cm (18in) long and 15cm (6in) wide. They have a broadly acuminate apex
and shortly dentate margin. The flower head contains yellow ray florets and
the petiole may be covered with long white hairs above. This striking plant

85

grows only on Mt Kenya and the Aberdares at 3,350–3,810m (11,000–12,500ft). Flower: panicle up to 1.3m (4ft) tall.

S.j. subsp. **barbatipes** is found only on Mt Elgon at 3,660–4,300m (12,000–14,100ft). Flower: panicle *c.* 1m (3¼ft) tall.

S.j. subsp. **cheranganiensis** occurs only on the Cheranganis at altitudes 2,600–3,400m (8,500–11,150ft). Flower: panicle up to 1m (3¼ft) tall.

S.j. subsp. **dalei** is found only on the Cheranganis at 3,050–3,400m (10,000–11,150ft). Flower: panicle *c.* 75cm (30in) tall.

S.j. subsp. **elgonensis** is also found only on Mt Elgon at altitudes 2,900–4,200m (9,400–13,755ft). Flower: panicle *c.* 1m (3¼ft) tall.

S. keniodendron is a species found only on Mt Kenya at altitudes 3,500–4,650m (11,500–15,250ft). Flower: inflorescence up to 1.3m (4ft) tall.

The following do not belong to subgenus Dendrosenecio

Senecio roseiflorus   **Plate 39** (247)
An erect herb or weak shrub with purple flowers which are open and daisy-like. It is locally common in the dryer alpine areas of Mt Kenya and the Aberdares at altitudes 2,900–4,000m (9,500–13,100ft). Flower head: *c.* 2cm (¾in) across.

Senecio syringifolius   **Plate 4** (27)
A dull grey-green, semi-succulent climber with twining stems and ovate or triangular leaves which often have lateral lobes at their base. Its flowers form a loose corymb without rays, cream, pale yellow, yellow or orange in colour. It is common in montane rain forest and the bamboo zone in Elgon, Mau, Aberdares, Mt Kenya, Kajiado, Machakos and the Chyulu Hills at 2,100–3,000m (6,700–9,850ft) and in the Chyulus extending down to 1,600m (5,250ft). Flower head: *c.* 7mm (¼in) across.

Sphaeranthus cyathuloides   **Plate 36** (227)
An erect, hairless, woody herb with narrow lanceolate-linear minutely serrate leaves and unwinged stems. Its pink inflorescence is conical and pointed at the apex. It is fairly common in wet places within grassland around Nairobi, in Machakos, and in Tsavo National Park at altitudes 500–1,800m (1,650–5,900ft). Inflorescence: *c.* 15mm (⅝in) long.

Sphaeranthus napierae   **Plate 36** (226)
A down-covered, trailing herb with ascending stems bearing elliptic, serrate leaves and subentire, continuous wings and with hairy, gradually-narrowing

COMPOSITAE

bracts. The rounded inflorescence is purple. It is a common endemic in fresh water in central and western Kenya at altitudes 1,450–2,000m (4,900–6,550ft). Flower head: *c.* 15mm (⅝in) diameter.

Sphaeranthus suaveolens* **Plate 37** (233)
A hairless, trailing herb with ascending stems bearing elliptic, serrate leaves and subentire, continuous wings. Its terminal inflorescence is round and purple. The smell of the leaves resembles apples. This is the commonest form of *Sphaeranthus*, found in or alongside fresh water all over Kenya at altitudes 1,220–2,500m (4,000–8,200ft). Flower head: *c.* 14mm (⅝in) across.

S. gomphrenoides is a weaker ascending herb with lanceolate leaves and interrupted stem wings. Its inflorescences are smaller than in *S. suaveolens* or *S. napierae*, paler in colour and more rounded at the apex. It is locally common in water courses and ephemeral pools in hotter country than either of the above, at altitudes of 760–1,200m (2,500–4,000ft).

Spilanthes mauritiana **Plate 15** (97)
A trailing herb with ovate, dentate leaves and small heads of rather bright, orange-yellow flowers with noticeable ray florets. It is a common plant in riverside grassland and in lawns in central and western Kenya at altitudes 610–2,500m (2,000–8,200ft). Flower head: 8mm (¼in) across.

Tagetes minuta **Plate 18** (118)
A weed from America which became common in East Africa after the First World War. It is an erect, strong smelling annual which is often robust but is very variable in habit with pinnate leaves having elliptic, serrate leaflets. Its creamy-yellow flower heads are grouped in terminal corymbs. It is an abundant and troublesome weed in upland farming areas and widespread in central Kenya from the Kitale area to Nairobi and Narok at altitudes 760–2,210m (2,500–7,250ft). Flower head: *c.* 5mm (¼in) across.

Taraxacum officinale **Plate 17** (108)
A virtually hairless herb with oblong, pinnatifid leaves and solitary yellow flowers. It is an introduction from Europe which was originally known only in the Limuru area in the altitude range 2,000–2,400m (6,500–7,900ft) but has now been found along the 2,300m (7,500ft) contour in the Aberdare region as far as upper Gilgil. Flower head: *c.* 25mm (1in) across.

Tarchonanthus camphoratus **Plate 4** (29)
This is the grey-leaved, medium-sized bush which the early European newcomers to Kenya called 'Leleshwa' (the Masai 'Olleleshwa') and associated with good, disease-free cattle country. It is a much-branched, dioecious shrub which grows to 6m (20ft) high. Its narrow, elliptic leaves have a short stalk and smell of camphor when crushed. Their margin is entire

87

COMPOSITAE

with the lamina green above and covered in dense white hairs beneath. The bell-shaped flower clusters form much-branched panicles of five to twelve grey-white flowers. The woolliness of the achenes gives the female inflorescence an appearance like cotton wool. It grows all over the floor of the Rift Valley and in parts of Kajiado and Narok. Reasonable tobacco pipes can be made from the roots and the stool shoots provide good knobkerries.

Tithonia diversifolia   **Plate 17** (109)
A branched, soft shrub with simple to five-lobed, opposite or alternate leaves and a large head of orange-yellow flowers. It can grow into a large bush. Introduced into East Africa from Central America, it is now common in west Kenya and on the western slopes of the Aberdares in hedgerows and waste ground, at altitudes 1,500–2,300m (5,000–7,500ft). It is also recorded in the Nairobi district. Flower head: 7cm (2¾in) across.

Vernonia auriculifera   **Plate 44** (283)
A large, tall-growing, woody shrub with grey hairs under the ovate, auriculate, petiolate leaves. Its very large corymb of flower heads is flat to slightly rounded, varying in colour from deep purple to medium mauve and fading to a pale violet. It is a prominent, widespread plant of the higher rainfall areas at altitudes of 1,070–3,000m (3,500–9,850ft) and is often a sign of fertile soil. Flower head: 3–4mm (*c.* ⅛in) across.

V. aemulans is an erect annual covered with soft hairs, often dense, which grows up to 1m (3¼ft) in height with oblanceolate to oblong leaves. Its purple flowers form rather flat solitary or corymbose flower heads. It is found in dry bushland and often on the edges of thickets bordering a road in the Embu, Machakos, Kajiado and Nairobi districts. Flower head: *c.* 11mm (⅜) across.

V. galamensis *(V. pauciflora)* is a large, erect, usually unbranched annual with elliptic to linear leaves and large terminal sometimes solitary scattered heads of blue-mauve florets. The phyllaries have a narrow to broad, recurved or spreading green appendage and the achenes are densely covered with soft hairs. It is a very variable robust annual with a wide ecological range growing in cleared dry woodland or forest, from 800–2,200m (2,600–7,200ft). It does not carry the great mauve-purple corymbose flower head of *V. auriculifera* but instead has medium-sized heads of mauve-blue florets rather like those of the garden 'Sweet Sultan'. At higher altitudes in montane forest areas, the flower heads are broader and there are broad recurved appendages on the phyllaries while the dry woodland form has bristle-like phyllaries and narrow heads and flowers. There are intermediates between these two types especially in the Nairobi area. The high altitude form has been given a separate name, *V. afromontana*. Both forms and intermediates are widespread throughout Kenya in their respective altitude ranges. Flower: *c.* 2cm (¾in) across.

47. GENTIANACEAE
The Gentian Family

A medium-sized, almost wholly herbaceous family. It is found mainly in temperate, or even arctic, climates but has some tropical representatives. These plants are almost always hairless, except sometimes for a few hairs on the corolla. Their leaves are opposite, without stipules and usually entire. The cymose inflorescences are formed of four to five regular flowers with a superior ovary of two united carpels. The fruit is usually a capsule with numerous seeds. There are 21 species in Kenya belonging to seven genera.

Swertia usambarensis   Plate 4 (26)
An erect, hairless herb with obovate basal leaves and linear to oblong stem leaves, branching above into a loose corymb of white flowers. The species is variable with short or long petals and is common in shallow soils and short montane grassland throughout Kenya at altitudes of 1,600–3,900m (5,250–12,800ft). Flower: c. 15mm ($\frac{5}{8}$in) across.

48. PRIMULACEAE
The Primrose Family

A medium-sized family of herbs found mainly in north temperate regions. Their leaves are simple and lack stipules. Flowers are usually regular, five in number and with their petals nearly always united. Five stamens are placed opposite the petals, the ovary is superior with numerous ovules of a central locus (free central placentation) and the fruit is a capsule. There are 15 species in Kenya belonging to five genera and nearly all are found at altitudes above 1,520m (5,000ft).

Anagallis serpens   Plate 34 (215)
A creeping or trailing plant with pink flowers which is a relative of the Pimpernel which grows in the cornfields of Europe. It is common in alpine and subalpine streamside marshes at altitudes 1,920–4,500m (6,300–14,750ft). Flowers: 5–15mm ($\frac{1}{8}$–$\frac{5}{8}$in) across.

49. PLUMBAGINACEAE
Sea Lavender Family

A rather small family of herbs or shrublets found in most parts of the world, especially in saline areas. Their leaves are alternate and lack stipules. The flowers are regular with a five-toothed, tubular calyx having five, ten or fifteen ribs. The corolla is tubular and often blue or purple. There are five stamens and a superior ovary with one ovule but five styles, or one style with five branches. The fruit is dry. There are six species in Kenya belonging to three genera.

Ceratostigma abyssinicum   Plate 47 (302)
A low, rough shrub with stiff, elliptic, sharply-pointed leaves and heads of blue flowers. A rare plant, it is found on dry rocky outcrops and scarps in the Northern Frontier and near Isiolo at altitudes of 700–1,500m (2,300–4,900ft) but no further south. Flower: *c.* 15mm ($\frac{5}{8}$in) across.

Plumbago zeylanica   Plate 7 (44)
A trailing, hairless shrub with ovate leaves and white flowers grouped in terminal spikes. It has a tubular calyx with stalked glands and a corolla with a long tube, *c.* 2cm ($\frac{3}{4}$in) long and spreading lobes. It is common in dry bushland throughout Kenya, up to an altitude of 2,000m (6,600ft) where rainfall is below 400mm (16in) per annum. Flower: *c.* 16mm ($\frac{5}{8}$in) across.

50.   CAMPANULACEAE (including Lobeliaceae)

The Harebell or Bell Flower Family

A medium-sized, mainly temperate climate family of herbs or, rarely, shrublets. Their leaves are nearly always alternate and without stipules. The flowers are usually blue and five in number: they are regular in the subfamily *Campanuloideae* and zygomorphic in the *Lobelioideae*. The stamens are separate in the *Campanuloideae* and connate in the *Lobelioideae*. The ovary is more or less inferior and the fruit a capsule opening by pores or, rarely, a berry. There are 36 species in Kenya belonging to six genera, nearly all found at altitudes above 1,220m (4,000ft).

Canarina abyssinica   Plate 27 (168, 169)
A dull grey-green climber with a fleshy rootstock and triangular, ovate leaves. Its pendulous, solitary flowers are orange-red with a five-lobed calyx and a large corolla which is tubular or bell-shaped. This beautiful plant is uncommon but well worth looking for. It is found in wet forests at altitudes of 1,620–2,130m (5,500–7,000ft), especially in western and central Kenya. Flower: 5–6cm (2–2$\frac{2}{5}$in) long.

C. eminii is very similar to *C. abyssinica*. It is usually, perhaps always, an epiphyte growing on trees and found at 1,980–2,290m (6,500–7,500ft) on Mt Elgon, Cheranganis, Tinderet, Mau, Aberdares and Mt Kenya.

Cyphia glandulifera   **Plate 40** (254)
A perennial herb of erect habit stemming from a buried tuber, which grows in
shallow soil. Its leaves grow in a rosette at the base. An attractive pink flower
with five petals appears immediately after the rains. It is usually borne on an
erect, straight stem, sometimes and especially in the Kedong Valley and on
the Rift Valley escarpment, on a twining stem. There is also a much-branched
form found generally in dry bushland. It is found over a wide area from the
Aberdare Highlands at an altitude of 1,900m (6,300ft) through districts such
as Rift Valley, Nairobi, and Kajiado to 700m (2,300ft) in areas such as lower
Machakos, and Baringo and is recorded as far east as Tsavo East National
Park. Flower: c. 1cm (⅜in) across.

Lobelia holstii   **Plate 39** (251)
A stiff perennial with ascending stems and oblanceolate, stalkless leaves.
Rather few flowers are borne at the top of a leafless flowering stem; they may
be reddish, purple or mauve (but not blue). It is the most common lobelia,
found in rocky places in dry grassland throughout central and eastern Kenya
at altitudes of 1,500–3,350m (5,000–11,000ft). Flower: c. 14mm (⅝in) long.

Lobelia keniensis   **Plate 48** (308)
A giant lobelia with a large, erect spike of blue-purple flowers that grows out
of a stemless rosette of leaves which often holds a pool of water. It is found
only on Mt Kenya, where it is common in marshes, above 3,050m (10,000ft).
Each high mountain area – Mt Elgon, Mt Kenya, the Aberdares, etc. – tends
to have its own specialised version of these tall lobelias. They nearly all have
the same form, a rosette of leaves with a single dominant spike, and tend to
grow in marshy places at altitudes above 2,130m (7,000ft), although the more
showy ones are found from 2,900m (9,500ft) upwards. Flower spike: 1m
(3¼ft) tall, 15cm (6in) in diameter.

Lobelia telekii   **Plate 48** (311)
A lobelia which is similar to *L. keniensis* and which grows to 4m (13ft) in
height. It has much narrower leaves than *L. keniensis* and its stem has long,
hairy, almost feathery, bracts which hang down and tend to hide the small
white and purple flowers. It is found in wet, stony ground on Mt Elgon, Mt
Kenya and the Aberdares at an altitude of 3,050m (10,000ft) or higher.
Flower spike: 1.6m (5ft) tall; 15cm (6in) in diameter.

Wahlenbergia abyssinica *(Lightfootia abyssinica)*   **Plate 46** (296)
The *Wahlenbergia* are erect herbs with alternate, simple leaves. The flowers
are either solitary or borne in racemes or corymbs and in most of the 13
species which have been recorded in Kenya are white or blue. This species,
however, has flowers which are more purple than blue. Wahlenbergia range
from alpine mountain zones to semi-arid areas such as Tsavo West where the
specimen illustrated was growing. Flower: corolla c. 1cm (⅖in) across.

51.   BORAGINACEAE (including Ehretiaceae)
The Forget-me-not Family

A medium-sized family of herbs, mainly of temperate zones but including a group of mainly tropical trees and shrubs (*Ehretioideae*). They usually have stiff and bristly hairs and their leaves are simple, nearly always alternate and lacking stipules. The flowers are usually regular, five in number and often blue or white. In the two woody genera, *Cordia* and *Ehretia*, which have 16 species in Kenya, the fruit is a drupe. In the eight herbaceous genera, which have about 32 species in Kenya, they have two or more, often four, dry nutlets. In all these herbaceous genera, except *Heliotropium*, the ovary consists of four loculi, each with a single ovule, which become four single-seeded nutlets, the style arising between them. This distinctive arrangement is found only here and in the *Labiatae*.

Cordia africana *(C. holstii, C. abyssinica)*   **Plate 3** (16)
A resplendent forest tree which generally reaches up to 10m (33ft) in height but can occasionally achieve the majesty of 24m (80ft). The stalkless flowers are most decorative, massed in white panicles. They are shorter than the leaves, white in colour and look as though they are made of paper. The strong ribbed calyx is a soft brown. This tree is widespread in forests at 1,040–2,100m (3,400–6,900ft), especially near Meru and Kakamega. Corolla: *c*. 25mm (1in) across.

Cynoglossum lancifolium   **Plate 46** (294)
An erect, perennial, downy herb with petiolate, ovate-elliptic lower leaves and stalkless upper ones. The rather large flowers are a bright blue. It is essentially a plant of montane forest areas at 2,250–3,300m (7,400–10,800ft) and often found in disturbed forest clearings and along the sides of banks of roads and tracks. In Kenya it is sometimes called the Forget-me-not but this name should be applied only to members of the related genus *Myosotis*, three species of which are found at high altitudes in Kenya. A related species is the Hound's tongue of European gardens, although it has quite different leaves which resemble a hound's tongue. Flower: corolla *c*. 9mm ($\frac{3}{8}$in) across.

C. amplifolium, an erect perennial herb covered with soft down with petiolate ovate-elliptic lower leaves and sessile upper ones, is a rarer species than *C. geometricum* and found principally near Uplands. The leaves are scabrid beneath when rubbed towards the apex. The large, bright blue flowers are in racemes like scorpiod cymes. The nutlets are uniformly spiney all over which distinguishes it from *C. lancifolium*, on which they are smooth except for a centre row of spines. Flower: 2–3mm (*c*. $\frac{1}{8}$in) across.

C. coeruleum is a trailing species, although sometimes it has a shrubby appearance. It is a rough-feeling perennial with linear leaves arranged in rosettes and small blue flowers. The seeds are usually spiny all over. It is common all over Kenya in upland grassland at the higher altitudes. Flower: 2–3mm (c. ⅛in) across.

C. geometricum An erect herb with entire leaves and bright blue flowers in raceme-like cymes which are coiled during development. The calyx is five-lobed, the corolla has a short tube and five spreading lobes and there are five stamens with short filaments. It is the most common Cynoglossum and widespread throughout Kenya in montane forest clearings, along the sides of paths and as a field weed at higher altitudes, 2,130–2,900m (7,000–9,500ft). Flower: c. 8mm (²⁄₁₆in) across.

Echiochilon lithospermoides   **Plate 45** (292)
An erect, woody annual with small, stalkless, ovate leaves and pink-mauve flowers. The leaves are an attractive blue-green. It is locally common in dry bushland in the Nanyuki and Kajiado districts. Flower: c. 5mm (⅕in) across.

Ehretia cymosa   **Plate 3** (18)
A tree which grows up to 18m (60ft) high that is usually found on the edge of forests. Its leaves are ovate, acute and entire and its white, stalkless flowers form many-flowered, down-covered, terminal panicles with the corolla not campanulate and three times the length of the calyx. This tree is widely distributed in areas of high rainfall, over 1,125mm (45in) per annum at altitudes of 1,220–1,830m (4,000–6,000ft). Flower: /mm (c. ¼in) across.

Heliotropium steudneri   **Plate 5** (30)
A perennial herb with elongating spikes of white or creamy-white flowers which is common almost everywhere from 1,100–2,250m (3,500–7,400ft), although preferring disturbed dry grassland alongside cut-off drains and old reverted fields. It is a relative of *H. peruvianum*, the Cherry Pie of gardens in Europe. Flower: c. 5mm (⅕in) across.

Heliotropium undulatifolium   **Plate 6** (37)
A bushy herb with short spikes of crowded creamy-white flowers and slightly hairy leaves. It is common in the drier, medium-altitude areas in grassland and along the sides of roads and tracks. Several other species of *Heliotropium*, in addition to this and *H. steudneri*, grow in their own habitats throughout Kenya. Flower: c. 7mm (c. ¼in) across.

52. SOLANACEAE

The Potato, Tobacco or Deadly Nightshade Family

A large family of erect or climbing herbs, shrubs or, very rarely, trees, found throughout the world but especially common in tropical America where *Solanum* alone has over 1,000 species. These plants are often poisonous. Their leaves are alternate and lack stipules. Their flowers are regular or slightly irregular with a tubular calyx, four- to five-toothed or lobed, sometimes inflated in fruit, and a four- to five-lobed corolla with the lobes induplicate-valvate. The fruit is a berry or a capsule, usually many-seeded. There are about 42 species in Kenya, belonging to eight genera, the so-called Irish Potato, *Solanum tuberosum* belongs to this family but the Sweet Potato, *Ipomoea batatas*, belongs to the Convolvulaceae.

Datura stramonium   **Plate 5** (33)
An erect, hairless annual with ovate, dentate leaves, dichotomously branched, with a white flower in the form of a small trumpet at each fork. It is widespread throughout Kenya at 600–2,300m (2,000–7,500ft) and travellers are sure to see it growing by roadsides everywhere and in disturbed patches and old cultivated ground. Its seeds are highly poisonous and can give rise to extreme hallucinations and excessive euphoria. It is an introduced weed, not indigenous to Kenya. Flower: *c.* 8cm (3in) long.

Nicotiana glauca   **Plate 14** (88)
An erect, loose shrub with ovate leaves on long stalks and yellow-orange flowers which have a corolla with a long narrow tube. It is not a truly indigenous plant but an escape from cultivation which is increasingly found wild in Nairobi and the Rift Valley near Naivasha at 1,520–2,130m (5,000–7,000ft). Flower: corolla 35mm (1¾in) long.

Solanum incanum   **Plate 44** (284)
An erect, felty-haired shrub, commonly known as the Sodom Apple, which often has prickles on its stem and stalks. Its leaves are ovate to lanceolate and entire to sinuate. The blue to mauve flowers are grouped in racemes. It is found all over Kenya in waste ground and along roadsides where the soil has been scraped away or eroded. It is less common over 2,300m (7,500ft). Flower: corolla *c.* 13mm (½in) across.

Solanum sessilistellatum   **Plate 43** (277)
A soft-haired perennial with prickles replacing hairs on its stem and leaves and lateral, almost stalkless umbels of pale purple flowers. Its leaves are alternate, simple or pinnately lobed, narrowing gradually at the base. It is a high altitude species found in clearings in montane forest at 2,390–3,050m (7,500–10,000ft). Flower: 27–50mm (1–2in) across.

SOLANACEAE

Solanum sp.* (from Chalbi Desert)   **Plate 44** (282)
There are more than 25 identified species of *Solanum* in Kenya which range
from small trees and shrubs to erect herbs and climbers and are often prickly.
Their flowers are blue to mauve or purple except for those noted above. In the
larger shrub-like species the fruit which is an irritant and poisonous takes the
form of a large yellow or pale yellow globe which has led to the name 'Sodom
Apple'. These plants are so varied in their leaf structure, habit and habitat
that it is best to pursue them in more detail in *Upland Kenya Wild Flowers*
where they are all comprehensively described.

S. aculeatissimum is similar to *S. sessilistellatum*, with pale purple flowers, but
has soft hairs on its stem and the upper side of its leaves and the inflorescence
is not stalked. Its distribution is similar to *S. sessilistellatum* but it can be also
found at lower levels, down to 1,830m (6,000ft) altitudes. Flower: *c.* 2cm ($\frac{3}{4}$in)
across.

S. giganteum is a loose shrub with spiny stems and oblanceolate entire leaves
and dense almost terminal corymbs of white flowers. It is an uncommon
plant found in wet montane forests in the Aberdares, Mt Kenya and the
Nyambeni Hills from 1,500–2,250m (5,100–7,400ft). Flower: corolla 13mm
($\frac{1}{2}$in) across.

S. nigrum is a soft erect, downy or hairless unarmed annual with elliptic entire
or crenate leaves; the inflorescence is extra-axillary and umbellate. The
flowers are white and the fruits orange or black. It is a very variable plant
which is a common weed in cultivated land below 2,100m (7,000ft) and grows
throughout Kenya from 5–2,700m (16–8,900ft). Flower: 4mm (*c.* $\frac{1}{8}$in) across.

S. nakurense is an erect unarmed herb or shrub from a trailing woody
rootstock with broad-elliptic, entire leaves and nearly terminal corymbs of
white to pale blue flowers. It is locally common in evergreen upland bushland
on Mt Elgon, the Cheranganis, Tinderet, Mau, the Aberdares, Kitale, Kisii,
Narok and Rift Valley, from 900–2,850m (3,000–9,350ft). Flower: *c.* 8mm
($\frac{2}{16}$in) across.

S. taitense is a prickly-stemmed weak and often supported shrub covered in
soft hairs with ovate pinnately-lobed leaves and small lateral sessile umbels of
one to two white or mauve flowers. It is locally common in dry acacia
bushland in Rift Valley, Magadi and Kajiado from 15–1,500m (50–5,000ft).
Flower: 10mm (*c.* $\frac{3}{8}$in) across.

53. CONVOLVULACEAE
The Bindweed, Morning Glory or Sweet Potato Family

A medium-sized family consisting mainly of twining plants, found throughout the world, but also including erect herbs, shrublets, shrubs and even trees. Their leaves are alternate, usually without stipules and entire, sometimes palmately lobed and, rarely, pinnate. The flowers are usually regular with the calyx five- (sometimes four-) partite and persistent. The corolla is usually funnel-shaped, unlobed or slightly five-lobed, or rarely, cylindrical. The ovary is superior, uni- to quadrilocular with one to four ovules in each loculus. The fruit may be a capsule or indehiscent and is most often four-seeded. There are 117 species in Kenya belonging to 20 genera. They include the *Cuscuta* which, apart from *Cassytha* in the Lauraceae are the only twining parasites found in Africa. There are 38 species of *Ipomoea* in Kenya.

Ipomoea cairica   **Plate 40** (258)
A common creeper with dissected leaves which is allied to the Morning Glory and Bindweed of European gardens. It generally has a pale mauve-pink flower but this can vary to white, with a darker throat. It is found in clearings in forests, swampy grassland, and hedges and on lake shores and waste and cultivated land at medium altitudes, 750–1,890m (2,460–6,200ft). Flower: *c.* 55mm (2⅛in) across.

Ipomoea cicatricosa   **Plate 37** (238)
This is an unusual *Ipomoea* in that it is a perennial erect shrub, not climbing or trailing, which grows to 1–2m (3–6ft) high. Its stems are covered with short dense down and its ovate or ovate-elliptic leaves, *c.* 7cm (2¾in) long and 4cm (1½in) wide, are hairless above and covered with soft, silky hairs pressed closely against their underside, especially when young. Its cymes are two- to three-flowered and axillary and the purple corollas are funnel-shaped. It is found in semi-arid areas at altitudes of 610–1,200m (2,000–4,000ft). Flower: corolla 25–30mm (1–1⅛in) across.

Ipomoea hederifolia   **Plate 28** (176)
An annual with hairless or sparsely-haired, twining stems. The leaves are ovate or rounded in outline, entire or three-lobed with margins entire, and angular or toothed. Inflorescences are often long and may be few- to several-flowered. The sepals have short bristle appendages and the scarlet corolla salver-shaped with the tube 28–40mm (1⅛–1⅝in) long and the expanded upper part 20–25mm (¾–1in) in diameter. A native of tropical America, it is now widely naturalised in Kenya and found in waste places, thickets and forest edges and on cliffs up to altitudes of 1,650m (5,400ft). It has been recorded in

CONVOLVULACEAE

western Kenya, Machakos, Nairobi and Meru and is quite common as an escape at the coast, but not in dry country. Flower: 20–25mm ($\frac{3}{4}$–1in) in diameter.

Ipomoea hildebrandtii   **Plate 40** (259)
A very variable, subwoody plant which grows up to 2.5m (8ft) in height with round to elliptic-oblong leaves which are covered with very fine down beneath and often large. The flowers may be few to many in dense to loose, branched cymes. The bracts and sepals are large; bracts 12–26mm ($\frac{1}{2}$–1in) long and 5–14mm ($\frac{3}{16}$–$\frac{5}{8}$in) wide and sepals 14–25mm (c. $\frac{1}{2}$–1in) long and 5–10mm ($\frac{3}{16}$–$\frac{3}{8}$in) wide; corolla purple, white or white with a purple tube and funnel-shaped, 4.5–11.5cm ($1\frac{3}{4}$–$4\frac{1}{4}$in) long. The seeds have dark, close-lying hairs. Three subspecies have been recognised, one with two varieties.

I. h. subsp. **hildebrandtii** photographed here, is found in eastern Kenya where it is common in grassland with scattered acacia and acacia-commiphora deciduous bushland, particularly along the Namanga road in the Narok and Kajiado districts, at altitudes 400–1,650m (1,300–5,400ft).

I. h. subsp. **grantii** is found in western Kenya and the Kisii districts in grassland and among scattered trees at 1,100–2,000m (3,500–6,500ft).

I. h. subsp. **grantii** var. **mahonii** with very narrow elliptic-oblong leaves occurs on Mt Elgon and in the Trans-Nzoia (Kitale) district at 1,950m (6,400ft).

I. h. subsp. **megaënsis** with an entirely purple corolla and more silky sepals than the other subspecies, is found in Nanyuki and Rumuruti districts and northwards to Mega in southern Ethiopia at 610–1,850m (2,000–6,050ft).

Ipomoea jaegeri   **Plate 42** (271)
A floriferous, erect shrub which grows to about 60cm (2ft) high with many stems. Its linear-oblong to oblong-oblanceolate leaves are green and slightly hairy above, silvery below. Funnel-shaped flowers are borne singly on short stalks and are white or pink with a darker centre. This beautiful non-climbing member of the Convolvulus family is common on stony soils, often along roadsides, in the Narok, Rift Valley, Magadi, Machakos, Nairobi and Kajiado areas at altitudes of 910–1,700m (3,000–5,600ft). Flower: c. 5cm (2in) across.

Ipomoea mombassana   **Plate 40** (257)
An annual or perennial twiner with hairy stems. Its leaves are ovate or ovate-oblong, or elongate-oblong, cordate, cordate-sagittate or subhastate-cordate, rough or hairy. The inflorescence is single- or several-flowered with the funnel shaped corolla purple or white with a purple centre and a narrow tube 3–5cm ($1\frac{1}{8}$–2in) long. This is a lowland species found in dry bushland

97

CONVOLVULACEAE

and commiphora and combretum woodland at altitudes up to 1,200m (4,000ft). Flower: 6cm (2⅓in) across.

Ipomoea obscura   **Plate 13** (87)
A small-flowered Ipomoea with an orange, bright yellow, cream or white corolla, always with a purple, crimson or chocolate-brown centre. It is common in dry or warm areas at 610–2,300m (2,000–7,500ft) over most of Kenya. Flower: *c*. 25mm (1in) across.

I. ochracea is almost exactly the same as *I. obscura* but has rather larger flowers. It is common over most of Kenya and is often found in forest strips, along river banks, in hot dry country and in commiphora bushland. Flower: corolla 2.4–4cm (*c*. 1–1½in) long.

Ipomoea spathulata   **Plate 41** (261)
A partly erect shrub with twining or scrambling branches which grows up to 2.5m (7½ft) long and is covered with grey or yellowish-grey hairs. Its leaves are a medium shade of green, thick and obtuse at the apex. Its flowers, several to many in number, are projected on short, branched cymes, the corolla being funnel-shaped and white or creamy-white with a darker mauve or purple centre from which pinkish-mauve rays project. This striking and handsome plant is found in north and central Kenya in districts with warm conditions at 1,200–2,100m (3,900–6,900ft). It can easily be grown from cuttings. Flower: corolla *c*. 5cm (2in) across.

Merremia sp.*   **Plate 22** (140)
A perennial or annual herb mostly with twining or creeping stems. The flowers are usually cream or yellow with a dark centre and are very similar to those of Ipomoea. The photograph shows an unidentified species on the East side of Lake Turkana (formerly L. Rudolph). Usually, Merremia species occur in semi arid or rocky conditions.

M. pinnata is an annual prostrate or trailing herb about 60cm (23½in) long with leaves sessile, deeply pinnatifid with 8–12 pairs of narrow lobes extending almost to the mid-rib about 8mm (⅓in) long, 0.5mm wide. There are one to three flowers which have a white to yellow corolla 7mm (slightly less than ⅓in) long. It is a widespread species in rocky grassland and bushland, especially in sandy soil. Altitude range 400–2,200m (1,300–7,200ft). Flower: 6mm (¼in) long.

M. ampelophylla is a perennial prostrate herb with radiating stems to about 1m (3ft 3in) in length. The leaves are palmately five- to seven-lobed, 2–8cm (¾–*c*. 3in) long and 3–14cm (1⅛–5½in) wide and usually undulate at margins. It has loose cymes of one to three flowers with primrose-yellow corollas and brownish-claret centres. It is found mostly in bare places in dry bushland.

98

SCROPHULARIACEAE

Altitude range 500–1,000m (1,650–3,300ft). Flower: corolla *c*. 3cm (1⅛in) long.

54. SCROPHULARIACEAE (including *Selaginaceae*)
The Foxglove Family

A large family of herbs or, rarely, shrubs, found throughout the world. Its leaves are opposite or alternate and without stipules. The flowers are usually zygomorphic with the more or less tubular calyx four- to five-lobed, usually four stamens, rarely, two or five, a bilocular ovary with numerous ovules attached to the septum and a long, single style. The fruit is a capsule with numerous minute seeds.

Many of the species of *Striga*, *Cycnium*, *Alectra* and *Bartsia* are parasites or semi-parasites which draw nourishment from the roots of grasses and perhaps other plants. Some species of *Striga* do very serious damage to cereals. There are 90 species of the family known in Kenya, belonging to 32 genera.

Craterostigma plantagineum   **Plate 45** (290)
A herb growing from a thick or thin rhizome with a basal rosette of spreading, broad-elliptic and often serrate leaves. Its blue to violet flowers are borne at the end of single stems and resemble violets. It is locally common on shallow soils in open sunny places and dry grassland, except in the very driest areas, over a wide area from Mumias in the west to Nanyuki in the east and from Mt Elgon to Kajiado, and especially common around Nairobi. It flowers very quickly and profusely as soon as the rains begin. Altitude range 1,600–2,200m (5,250–7,200ft). Flower: *c*. 7mm (¼in) across.

C. pumilum is similar in leaf growth to *C. plantagineum* but is shorter and has long blue to pinkish flowers at the end of single stems. It grows mainly around 2,130m (7,000ft) altitude in high dry grassland areas such as those of Mt Elgon, Cheranganis, Tinderet, Aberdares, Mau and Nanyuki and like the preceding species flowers profusely on the arrival of the rains. Altitude range 1,000–3,000m (3,300–9,900ft). Flower: 13mm (*c*. ½in) across.

C. hirsutum is a short, silky and hairy herb with an erect rosette of elliptic to obovate leaves and long racemes of flowers which are usually white. It is abundant in shallow soils and seasonal wet pans or flooded areas in short grassland. It is found in most of central and eastern Kenya, including the Rift Valley, but not in western districts, at 350–2,250m (1,100–7,400ft). Flower: 7mm (¼in) across.

Cycnium cameronianum *(Rhamphicarpa cameroniana)*   **Plate 36** (232)
An erect, although low, annual with down-covered stems and deeply serrate

99

leaves. Its flowers are bright pink. It is abundant after rains in dry commiphora bushland in districts such as Magadi, Machakos and Kajiado at 610–1,350m (2,000–4,500ft). Flower: *c.* 25mm (1in) across.

C. veronicifolium is rather similar in appearance. It is found in the coastal province.

Cycnium tubulosum subsp. **montanum** *(Rhamphicarpa montana)*
Plate 31 (199)
Like all cycniums a semi-parasitic plant which draws nourishment from the roots of the grasses to which it is attached. It is frequently a hairless, erect or ascending perennial herb from a fibrous rootstock with linear-lanceolate, often sparsely-toothed leaves. Its large pink or white flowers are borne on individual stalks in a loose raceme and are often only a few in number. It is a very variable species with some tall erect forms with many-flowered racemes, which are found principally in western Kenya. The form with few flowers and ascending stems which is found in the Nairobi district often seems to grade into *C. montanum* which is widespread in Kenya on black cotton grassland soils at 910–2,410m (3,000–7,900ft). It is common after rain in the Masai Mara area and looks like pieces of waste paper dotted across the plains. Flower: 4–5cm (2in) across.

Ghikaea speciosa **Plate 38** (241)
A stiffly erect bushy plant, *c.* 1.5m (4½ft) tall which is found in dry areas in acacia-commiphora bushland at 450–1,200m (1,500–4,000ft) and has mauve flowers. It is the only known species in this genus and has been recorded in northeastern Kenya and Somalia. Flower: 2–3cm ($\frac{3}{4}$–1¼in) across.

Hebenstretia dentata **Plate 6** (38)
A small, erect, wiry shrub with terminal spikes of white and orange flowers. It is common in rocky heathland at high altitudes up to 4,000m (13,120ft) but can also occasionally be found in dry grassland at 1,700–2,450m (5,500–8,000ft). It has been identified in Mt Elgon, Cheranganis, Aberdares, Mt Kenya, Rift Valley and Kajiado areas. Flower: corolla 2–3mm (*c.* ⅛in) across.

Pseudosopubia hildebrandtii **Plate 32** (206)
An erect or prostrate, down-covered, woody herb with linear, acute or obtuse leaves and loose terminal racemes of purple-pink flowers. It is common in dry bushland in northern and eastern Kenya at 690–1,300m (300–4,250ft) and, rarely, up to 1,650m (6,400ft). This species is variable and may one day be classified into three or four separate species. Flower: 15mm (⅝in) across.

Striga asiatica is an erect downy rough-skinned annual root parasite with linear to filamentous leaves and bright crimson flowers in a terminal spike.

This is a conspicuous plant found in upland and dry lowland grassland from sea level to 2,300m (7,600ft) and recorded throughout Kenya, except in dry and arid areas. Especially in Western Kenya and in Siaya district it is sometimes a bad parasitic weed on maize and sorghum plants. Flower: *c.* 16mm (⅝in) long and 7mm (*c.* ¼in) across.

Verbascum sinaiticum   **Plate 18** (116)
An erect, woolly herb 120–150cm (4–5ft) high, springing from a rosette of large ovate to oblong leaves and bearing simple or branched, terminal racemes of yellow flowers. It is a showy species most common in regions of medium rainfall, especially in wheat lands and along the sides of roads at 1,900–2,750m (6,200–9,000ft) and recorded in Tinderet, Mau, Aberdares, Rift Valley, Nanyuki and Timau districts. Flower: *c.* 1cm (⅜in) across.

Veronica abyssinica   **Plate 47** (304)
A trailing, down-covered herb with ovate, cordate and serrate leaves. It bears two- to five-flowered racemes of large blue-mauve flowers. It is common in upland grassland and forest edges and widespread in Kenya from 1,550–3,900m (5,100–12,800ft). Flower: 8mm (*c.* ¼in) across.

55. OROBANCHACEAE

The Broomrape Family

A small family of root parasites, found mainly in temperate regions. They are almost devoid of chlorophyll and closely related to the *Scrophulariaceae*, from which they differ chiefly in the ovary. This is unilocular with the very numerous ovules attached to four perietal placentas. There are four species in Kenya belonging to two genera.

Cistanche tubulosa   **Plate 12** (74)
An erect, unbranched spike of yellow flowers, rather like a large hyacinth, which is a parasite of shrubs and trees. Its base is always growing on their roots. It is locally common in dry and open bushland, mainly at low altitudes, 600–1,200m (2,000–4,000ft) and often found springing from the ground in open spaces. Flower: *c.* 12mm (½in) across when open.

Orobanche minor is an erect sparsely branched root parasite with pale dirty white to purple flowers in terminal spikes and the calyx split above and below the flower. The inflorescence is carried on a long erect peduncle from a base of leaves reduced to scales chiefly near the base of the stem. It is common in cultivated ground, upland grassland, forest edges and is widespread in Kenya though no specimen has been recorded in the Northern Frontier areas and Turkhana except one from Moyale, parasitic on maize. Altitude range from 800–2,400m (2,600–7,900ft). Flower: *c.* 15mm (⅝in) across.

56. GESNERIACEAE

The African Violet Family

A medium-sized almost wholly tropical or subtropical, family of herbs or much less often shrubs, climbers or trees. They differ from the *Scrophulariaceae* chiefly in the ovary, which is two-celled below but one-celled above with numerous ovules on two placentas intruding from the central division. There are eight species in Kenya belonging to two genera.

Streptocarpus exsertus Plate 4 (28)
A rare plant which is only known to occur on two basement complex mountains in northern Kenya where it is found in moist shady crevices at 1,430–1,520m (4,700–5,000ft). It was first discovered in 1963 and described scientifically in 1971. The basement complex mountains support a number of plants which are different from those found on the more prominent volcanic mountains, not only because the soils are more sandy and poorer in certain minerals but also because they existed long before the volcanoes appeared.

The specimen illustrated is shown in a pot because when first located on Ol Lolokwe it was not in flower and was, therefore, transplanted and grown on until the white flower could be photographed. Flower: *c.* 7mm ($\frac{1}{4}$in) long.

57. BIGNONIACEAE

A medium-sized family of tropical trees, climbers and shrubs, most common in America. Their leaves are nearly always opposite, usually pinnate, less often palmate or simple and sometimes end in tendrils. The corolla tube of the zygomorphic flowers is bell-shaped, funnel bell-shaped or tubular. The stamens usually number four and the ovary is superior, bi-locular and has numerous ovules. The fruit is a capsule or drupe. There are nine species in Kenya belonging to five genera. They include the Nandi Flame Tree and the *Jacaranda.*

Kigelia africana *(K. aethiopica)* Plate 30 (189)
A low-branched tree, commonly known as the Sausage Tree, which grows to 9m (30ft) in height. Its leaves are paired and opposite, the elliptic-oblong leaflets, usually seven to nine in number, are rounded at the base and 625–150mm (2$\frac{1}{2}$–5in) long. The unpleasantly scented flowers have a trumpet shaped corolla, the inside reddish or maroon, the outside pale with reddish lines. The fruit hangs down like a long sausage – hence the tree's popular name. It is widely spread in warm and wet savannah country and along rivers in dry areas up to altitudes of 1,830m (6,000ft). Flower: corolla up to 12cm (4$\frac{1}{2}$in) long.

58. ACANTHACEAE

A large tropical family of herbs, shrublets or, rarely, shrubs with a few warm temperate representatives. Their leaves are opposite, without stipules, nearly always simple, usually entire and usually containing dark crystalline bodies called cystoliths. The bracts are often conspicuous in the inflorescence. There are four or five sepals, free or slightly united, a zygomorphic corolla, usually five-lobed, and two or four stamens. The ovary is superior, bi-locular and usually has two (although sometimes one or three) ovules per loculus. The style is terminal and often bilobed. The fruit is a capsule, usually containing about four flat seeds. A few genera with more numerous ovules and seeds form a transition to the *Scrophulariaceae*. There are about 150 species in Kenya belonging to 35 genera.

Acanthus eminens   **Plate 47** (303)
A woody herb with royal blue flowers which grows to a height of 3m (10ft). Its large thistle-like leaves are opposite, oblong-elliptic and deeply pinnatifid or lobate with spiny margins. They may be up to 30cm (12in) long and 15cm (6in) wide, although they can be only half this size. This herb is found at 1,830–2,770m (6,000–9,100ft) covering large areas in cedar and allied forest. Flower: *c*. 5cm (2in) long.

A. pubescens *(A. arboreus)* is much taller than *A. eminens*, up to 6m (20ft) in height and more vigorous. Its inflorescence is rose, pink or magenta. It is found in western Kenya at 1,125–1,800m (3,700–6,000ft). *A. arboreus* is now considered to be confined to the Yemen only. Flower: *c*. 35mm (1⅜in) across.

Barleria acanthoides   **Plate 1** (1)
A small, low growing shrub having elliptic to oblong, spathulate leaves with markedly-toothed spines, often as long as the leaves, which spring from the point where the leaf joins the stem. The white flowers, often single, open at night from a long cylindrical tube. They are pollinated by moths with long tongues. In the morning they turn blue-black in colour and die when the sun becomes hot about 11.00 hours. This delightful species grows in dry scrub, bushland and semi-arid grassland, often in rocky places and generally at altitudes of 60–1,550m (200–5,100ft) in the Narok, Baringo, Magadi, Machakos and Kajiado districts. Flower: corolla tube *c*. 4cm (1⅝in) long; corolla *c*. 2cm (¾in) across.

Barleria eranthemoides   **Plate 10** (63)
A small, much-branched, spiny shrub with almost stalkless, elliptic leaves and spines between the stalks. The flowers are yellow to orange in dense, spiny heads. The corolla tube is cylindrical and narrow with a subequally five-lobed limb. It is found in dry grassland and bushland at 150–1,800m

(500–5,900ft) in Narok, Baringo, Magadi, Machakos and Kajiado districts and in all drier areas. Flower: *c.* 18mm ($\frac{3}{4}$in) across.

Barleria spinisepala   Plate 46 (295)
A low growing, much-branched, woody perennial herb with almost stalkless, elliptic, mucronate leaves and pinnatisect spines between the stalks. Its solitary flowers are axillary with a spiny-margined calyx and a pale blue corolla. It is night-flowering and by midday the corolla has dropped. It is found in dry grassland, especially in northern Kenya and the eastern Masai country (Kajiado district) at 1,500–2,150m (4,900–7,000ft) rarely at lower altitudes. Flower: corolla *c.* 2cm ($\frac{3}{4}$in) across.

Barleria submollis   Plate 40 (256)
An erect or semi-prostrate herb which sometimes roots at the nodes. Its leaves are obtuse and rounded at the base. Its blue flowers are axillary and grow in clusters of one to three. It is found in savannah and bushland at 900–1,350m (3,000–4,500ft). Flower: corolla *c.* 15mm ($\frac{5}{8}$in) across.
    There are many other species of Barleria in Kenya at low and medium altitudes with white, yellow or blue flowers. They are difficult to classify and much work still needs to be done on them.

Blepharis linariifolia   Plate 46 (298)
A prostrate annual plant with stalkless, unequally indented, spine-toothed leaves. Its elongated terminal spikes, short at first, bear bright blue flowers. It is found in open spaces in dry thornbush and grassland in northeastern and southern Kenya, especially in the Northern Frontier and near Voi, at altitudes of 140–1,400m (450–4,600ft). Flower: *c.* 18mm ($\frac{3}{4}$in) long.

Brillantaisia nitens   Plate 41 (264)
An erect, much-branched, perennial herb, growing to 2m ($6\frac{1}{2}$ft) high, with broadly ovate, acuminate, evenly serrate leaves, narrowing sharply below into the winged petiole and rarely cordate. The flowers are in a long, narrow panicle with the upper bracts elliptic to oblanceolate and with large blue-purple corollas. It is found in western Kenya from Kericho to Kitale in forest undergrowth at 1,650–2,200m (5,400–7,200ft). Flower: *c.* 26mm (1in) long.

Crossandra nilotica   Plate 27 (174)
A short, erect, sometimes straggling, branched herb with elliptic-lanceolate leaves and spikes of red or apricot flowers. It is found in partial shade in wooded grassland and dry bushland and occasionally in olive forest at 1,070–2,400m (3,500–8,000ft) in Tinderet, Kisii, Rift Valley, Narok and Baringo districts. Inflorescence: *c.* 35mm ($1\frac{3}{8}$in) across.

Crossandra subacaulis   Plate 32 (202)
A low growing plant with leaves crowded almost into a rosette. The apricot to

ACANTHACEAE

orange, or even red, spikes of closely-knit flowers spring from the leaves only a few inches or centimetres above the ground. It grows in savannah country, open grassland and on rocky slopes up to 1,690m (5,500ft) in the Nairobi, Machakos, Narok and Kajiado districts and is fairly common on stony slopes in the Maasai Mara area. Inflorescence: *c.* 5cm (2in) across.

C. friesiorum is similar to *C. tridentata* but found at 1,220–1,500m (4,000–5,000ft). Flower: 17–21mm (*c.* $\frac{3}{4}$in) across.

C. mucronata has pale orange to red flowers and is found in dry areas up to 1,800m (6,000ft). Flower: 18–26mm (*c.* $\frac{3}{4}$–1in) across.

C. stenostachya has yellow flowers and is found at altitudes up to 910m (3,000ft) in the Machakos district in grassland and wet places in arid areas. Flower: 10–12mm ($\frac{3}{8}$–$\frac{1}{2}$in) across.

C. tridentata is generally a straggling plant with small white flowers found in dense shade in forest or damp forest undergrowth up to altitudes of 2,450m (8,000ft). Flower: 11mm (*c.* $\frac{3}{8}$in) across.

Dyschoriste sp.*   **Plate 32** (203)
An erect herb or shrub with entire or obscurely crenate leaves and axillary cymes of pale mauve or purple flowers. Bracts and bracteoles are linear and much smaller than the calyx. It is locally common in disturbed or wooded grassland at medium altitudes and widespread both in Kenya and Tanzania. There are seven species of *Dyschoriste* recorded in Upland Kenya (i.e. above 900m or approximately 3,000ft in altitude) but as field material was not available, the photograph records one which has not been identified. Flower: *c.* 10mm ($\frac{3}{8}$in) long.

Ecbolium revolutum   **Plate 47** (307)
A small shrub with ovate to elliptic, acute or rounded leaves and blue or occasionally white, flowers in spikes up to 8cm (3in) long. It has minute down on all its parts, although the leaves are almost hairless. It is locally common in fine soils in dry bushland and has been recorded in Magadi, Machakos and Kajiado districts and in Tsavo East National Park, where it grows alongside *E. hamatum*. Flower: *c.* 12–16mm (*c.* $\frac{1}{2}$–$\frac{5}{8}$in) across.

E. hamatum has similarly-coloured but longer spikes than *E. revolutum*, up to 12cm (4$\frac{3}{4}$in) in length, and has no minute down. It is common in the Samburu district at 150–1,700m (500–5,600ft) and also found in Tsavo East National Park. Flower: *c.* 15mm ($\frac{5}{8}$in) across.

Hypocstes verticillaris   **Plate 41** (260)
A very variable, straggling or erect, perennial herb with elliptic leaves. The

105

flowers, borne in the axils of the peduncle, are pale mauve streaked with pink, purple or white, or sometimes all white. Because it is so variable it can be found in a wide range of habitats in bushland, dry grassland, forest edges and clearings from 10–2,740m (30–9,000ft). Flower: 14mm ($\frac{1}{2}$in) long.

H. aristata is rather similar to *H. verticillaris* with lanceolate leaves and axillary whorls of white, pink or mauve flowers, which are neither as close together nor as dense as those of *H. verticillaris*. It is found in forest, thicket or in the margins of relict forest patches in most parts of Kenya at altitudes 1,250–2,710m (4,100–8,900ft). Flower: 13mm (*c.* $\frac{1}{2}$in) long; 6mm (*c.* $\frac{1}{4}$in) across.

Justicia diclipteroides   **Plate 41** (263)
A sparsely pubescent, trailing herb which roots at the nodes. It has ovate leaves and scattered purple to pink flowers in the upper axils. It is a common species in evergreen forest edges in eastern Kenya, found at 1,220–2,130m (4,000–7,000ft) in eastern Mau, Aberdares, Narok, Nanyuki, Embu, Macha-kos, Nairobi and Kajiado districts. The common upland form around Nairobi has tightly downward curved stem hairs and in dry bushland there is a form with spreading, mixed glandular and eglandular stem hairs. Flower: *c.* 8mm ($\frac{3}{8}$in) across.

Justicia flava   **Plate 12** (80)
A trailing or erect, downy, woody herb with ovate, acute leaves and crowded terminal spikes of yellow flowers subtended by oblong to lanceolate bracts. It is common in a variety of open habitats and over a wide ecological range and found almost everywhere in its habitat in Kenya up to an altitude of 2,200m (7,200ft). A very variable species. Flower: *c.* 6mm ($\frac{1}{4}$in) across.

Justicia sp.*   **Plate 38** (246)
There are more than 25 recorded species of *Justicia* in Kenya; some are erect and others trailing and the flowers can be white, pink, mauve or purple, according to the species. The altitude range is 900–2,100m (3,000–7,000ft). Only *J. flava* described and shown above has yellow flowers. The photograph shows an unidentified species as field material was not available. Flower: average size 3–15mm ($\frac{1}{8}$–$\frac{3}{5}$in) long.

Phaulopsis imbricata   **Plate 4** (24)
A down-covered, trailing herb with ascending stems bearing elliptic leaves which gradually narrow at the base and apex. The flowers are small and form dense, one-sided, lateral or terminal spikes with white corollas. It is common on the floor of drier forests and in evergreen woodland everywhere in Kenya at altitudes of 1,520–2,450m (5,000–8,000ft). Flower: corolla, over 8mm ($\frac{1}{3}$in) long.

ACANTHACEAE

Ruttya fruticosa   **Plate 26** (164)
A shrub which can grow up to a height of 3m (10ft) but is often smaller. Its leaves are entire, ovate or elliptic and up to 5cm (2in) long. The markedly two-lipped flowers are coppery red with a splash of black in the throat. It is recorded over most of central, southern and northern Kenya in moderately dry bushland and forest margins, especially on rocky ground, at 610–1,825m (2,000–6,000ft). It is commonly cultivated as an ornamental shrub and a yellow variety is also grown in gardens. Flower: *c*. 2cm ($\frac{3}{4}$in) long.

Thunbergia alata   **Plate 24** (151)
A climbing or trailing plant, popularly known as 'Black-eyed Susan'. Its slightly hairy leaves are triangular to lanceolate or ovate. The flowers, often borne in considerable numbers, are usually orange but sometimes local forms are red, white or yellow. They have a purple centre and tube, this is sometimes very dark in colour, leading to the common name. It is found up to an altitude of 2,740m (9,000ft) in bushland, thicket and secondary grassland over many districts, usually in partial shade. It prefers wetter, higher altitude zones for full vigour and can then often be seen covering or half covering a large bush. Flower: *c*. 4cm ($1\frac{1}{2}$in) across.

T. battiscombei is an erect shrub, rarely climbing except in semi bush shade or woodland, which has large lilac flowers with an orange or yellow throat. It frequents savannah and grassland at 1,070–2,300m (3,500–7,500ft) in Mt Elgon, Kitale and Kisii districts. Flower: corolla 4.5cm ($1\frac{3}{4}$in) long. The mouth of tube 1.4cm (*c*. $\frac{5}{8}$in) wide and flower *c*. 3cm ($1\frac{1}{8}$in) across

Thunbergia gregorii   **Plate 25** (159)
A trailing herb which has orange hairs on its stems and peduncles. The leaves are broadly lanceolate-triangular and it bears solitary deep orange flowers on long stalks. It is apparently very local and is found in upland grassland at 1,800–2,300m (5,800–7,500ft) in Kisii, Machakos, Kajiado and Nairobi and especially in the Ngong Hills. Flower: *c*. 45mm ($1\frac{3}{4}$in) across.

Thunbergia guerkeana   **Plate 5** (32)
A climber with white tubular flowers which open at night and are presumably visited by long-tongued moths. It is common in most dry bushland areas at altitudes of 400–1,100m (1,300–3,600ft). The ten- to twelve-lobed calyxes form whitish-green, star-like structures which are hidden in the bud by two large bracts, as in all species of *Thunbergia*. These are clearly seen in our illustration. Flower: *c*. 10cm (4in) long.

Thunbergia holstii   **Plate 45** (289)
A medium-sized, bush-like shrub with lovely trumpet-shaped, solitary flowers which are bluish-purple with a yellowish centre. It grows in profusion in wooded grassland and bushland up to an altitude of 1,500m (5,000ft) and

VERBENACEAE

is common in Magadi, Embu, Nairobi, Machakos and Kajiado districts. It can be seen to perfection along the Ngulia mountain range in Tsavo West. Flower: *c.* 25mm (1in) across.

59. VERBENACEAE

The Teak Family

A medium-sized family of mainly tropical trees, shrubs or herbs. Their leaves are usually simple, opposite or whorled and lack stipules. The calyx is five-lobed and more or less tubular, the corolla zygomorphic (sometimes obscurely so) and the stamens number four. The ovary of two fused carpels is two- to four-locular with one ovule in each loculus, the style is terminal and the fruit divides into two or more parts. There are about 70 species in Kenya of which 45 are trees or shrubs. They belong to 13 genera.

Chascanum hildebrandtii   **Plate 2** (10)
A perennial herb from a woody rootstock which has long-stalked, obovate to elliptic leaves and spikes of white flowers. It is common in some areas of dry commiphora or combretum woodland, especially in sandy or disturbed places at altitudes 14–1,800m (45–5,900ft) in the Baringo, Magadi, Nanyuki, Embu, Machakos and Kajiado districts, the Tsavo National Parks and widespread in the Northern Frontier. Flower: *c.* 25mm (1in) long.

Clerodendrum myricoides   **Plate 44** (285)
A shrub growing to about 2.5m (8ft) in height with almost stalkless leaves which are arranged in whorls around the stem and ovate to elliptic with acute apex, deeply-toothed margin and cuneate base. Its irregular flowers, grouped in few-flowered cymes, form a terminal panicle. The calyx is sparsely-hairy or hairless with rounded lobes, obtuse and erect. The very short corolla tube has white or pale blue, obovate upper lobes and slightly longer, spathulate lower lobes which are dark blue. This shrub is found in bushland and forest margins at 1,500–2,400m (5,000–8,000ft) in all except the driest areas of Kenya. Flower: *c.* 15mm ($\frac{5}{8}$in) across.

Clerodendrum rotundifolium   **Plate 3** (15)
A shrub with densely down-covered twigs which grows to 2.5m (8ft) in height. Its leaves are opposite or ternate, ovate to suborbicular, downy, and up to 15cm (6in) long and broad, with margins entire or crenate, base rounded or cordate. Its regular, white flowers form loose, few-flowered, long-stalked terminal cymes. The calyx is 12mm ($\frac{1}{2}$in) long and the slender corolla tube 76mm (3in) long. It is found in the wetter districts of Meru, Kericho, Mt Elgon, Nandi and Sotik at 1,200–2,150m (4,000–7,000ft).

Lantana camara **Plate 31** (197)
A herbaceous shrub with opposite or ternate, roughish, stalked leaves. It has prickly stems and rather showy, large, pinkish-mauve flowers which can also bear touches of orange and white. It is certain to be noticed in all average or above average rainfall areas at 5–1,800m (15–6,000ft) pushing its way through the bush and forming large dense thickets. This is an introduced species and almost a noxious weed and is sometimes known as the Curse of India. Flower: *c.* 3mm ($\frac{1}{8}$in) across.

Lippia javanica **Plate 8** (54)
An erect, down-covered shrub with lanceolate to oblong leaves which usually has more than four narrow spikes to each node. The white flowers are on pedunculate, crowded spikes; the calyx small, two- to four-lobed and two-keeled. The corolla has four white or cream lobes and the stamens are included in the corolla tube. The underside of the leaves is covered with dense white down. It is widespread throughout the upland areas of Kenya at 1,280–2,200m (4,200–7,200ft) and abundant in disturbed places and rocky soils in dry woodlands. Flower head: 6mm ($\frac{1}{4}$in) across. Flower: 2mm (*c.* $\frac{1}{16}$in) across.

L. ukambensis is very similar to *L. javanica*, with white flowers, but is rough, not downy, on the underside of the leaves. It is an abundant invader of disturbed places and rocky soils in dry woodland throughout Kenya from 1,300–2,200m (4,250–7,200ft). Flower head: 12mm (*c.* $\frac{1}{2}$in) across. Flower: 3–4mm (*c.* $\frac{1}{8}$in) across.

Verbena bonariensis **Plate 37** (239)
An erect, often robust, downy annual which often attains a height of 2m (6$\frac{1}{2}$ft). It has stalkless, oblong, serrate leaves and carries large terminal corymbs of short spikelets with violet-purple flowers. It is often seen, mainly east of the Mau Escarpment, except in the Tinderet area, along the sides of roads and on the edges of forest at altitudes 1,620–2,440m (5,500–8,000ft). It is not a true native of East Africa, being introduced from South America. Flower: *c.* 4mm (*c.* $\frac{1}{6}$in) across.

60.   LABIATAE (Lamiaceae)

The Dead Nettle, Mint or Sage Family

A large family of usually aromatic herbs, shrublets or shrubs found in both temperate and tropical countries. Their leaves are opposite, rarely with entire margins, and usually aromatic, containing oil glands which, under a lens, can often be seen as dots. They have quadrangular stems and a tubular calyx which is often zygomorphic. The corolla is nearly always zygomorphic and

109

nearly always two-lipped. There are four stamens, or two in a few genera, either arched up under the lip in the more temperate genera, such as *Leonotis, Leucas, Nepeta, Salvia* and *Satureia* or bent downwards in the lower lip in the tropical *Plectranthus* and related genera. They have an ovary with four one-seeded portions surrounding the base of the style, which become four nutlets in the fruit. There are some 140 species in Kenya belonging to 32 genera.

Achyrospermum carvalhi   **Plate 30** (191)
An erect, soft shrub, covered with short, soft hairs below the elliptic, acute and attenuate leaves and bearing short racemes of bright red, long-tubed flowers. It is a rare plant found at 1,600–2,100m (5,250–6,900ft) altitudes and was recorded only on Mt Kenya until the specimen illustrated was discovered in the Mathews Range. Flower: *c.* 15mm ($\frac{5}{8}$in) across.

Becium obovatum   **Plate 1** (5)
An erect or trailing, down-covered or hairless herb or wiry shrub which grows from a woody rootstock or rhizome. Its leaves are oblong, obovate or ovate and rounded at the base or at the apex. It bears head-like inflorescences of white or pale pink flowers. It is common in upland grassland, appears to grow where drainage is poor and is very variable. It has been recorded at 300–2,400m (1,000–7,750ft) over most of eastern and central Kenya. Flower: including stamen, *c.* 16mm ($\frac{5}{8}$in) long.

Becium sp. A   **Plate 1** (6)
An erect, often woody annual with elliptic to lanceolate, acute, downy leaves and long, interrupted racemes of white to pale pink flowers. It is locally common in dry rocky country in Kisii, Machakos, Embu, Magadi, Kajiado and northern areas at altitudes 460–1,370m (1,500–4,500ft). Flower: *c.* 17mm ($\frac{5}{8}$in) long.

Erythrochlamys spectabilis   **Plate 39** (252)
An erect, downy shrub with oblong-lanceolate, almost stalkless leaves and simple terminal racemes of purple flowers. The calyx becomes very enlarged and conspicuous and bright red in fruit. It is found mostly below 1,000m (3,200ft) and is common in disturbed dry sandy bushland, although not in the very driest areas, in Machakos, Embu and Northern Frontier districts. It is especially common in the Voi-Kibwezi area at 300–1,350m (1,000–4,500ft). Flower: corolla *c.* 10mm ($\frac{3}{8}$in) long; 5mm ($\frac{3}{16}$in) across. Fruiting calyx: *c.* 1cm ($\frac{2}{5}$in) across.

Geniosporum rotundifolium *(G. paludosum)*   **Plate 35** (224)
An erect herb from a woody rootstock which branches above with short-stalked, ovate to oblong leaves and terminal racemes of small, pinkish flowers subtended by large white bracts at the base of the racemes. It is found mainly in marshes in western Kenya from Kitale through Elgon and the

110

Cheranganis to Tinderet, western Mau and Kisii at altitudes of 1,500–2,800m (4,900–9,200ft). Inflorescence: *c.* 1cm ($\frac{3}{8}$in) across.

Leonotis mollissima   **Plate 24** (153)
An erect, woody herb or shrub which sometimes reaches tree-like propor-
tions. Its leaves are woolly, ovate and cordate and its orange, or occasionally
white, flowers are grouped in one to three terminal spherical masses. This is
the common *Leonotis* above 1,950m (6,500ft) where it can be seen at the side
of roads, in disturbed places and often in montane forest. Although its
overall altitude range is 1,200–2,600m (3,900–8,500ft) it is rare in the lower
altitudes where it tends to be supplanted by *L. nepetifolia*. Both are much
favoured by sunbirds. Flower: *c.* 25mm (1in) long.

Leonotis nepetifolia   **Plate 24** (154)
A down-covered, tall-growing, erect, woody annual with long petiolate
leaves and orange flowers grouped in spherical masses at intervals up the
stem. It is the common *Leonotis* at lower altitudes, found all over Kenya up to
2,100m (7,000ft) almost as a weed. Flower: *c.* 25mm (1in) long.

L. leonurus a woolly, erect species also has orange flowers. Its leaves are never
wider than 4cm (*c.* 1½in). It grows on dry hillsides in the Aberdares, Mau, Rift
Valley, Machakos and Kajiado districts at medium altitudes up to 2,100m
(7,000ft). Flower: corolla 35mm (1$\frac{3}{8}$in) long.

Leucas urticifolia   **Plate 3** (19)
An erect, woolly, often powdery, short-lived herb or shrub, with ovate-
elliptic leaves and rather large round clusters of hairy, white flowers up the
stem. It is a common flower on old cultivated land, hut sites and disturbed
ground generally in dry country in the Nanyuki, Embu, Kajiado and
Northern Frontier districts at altitudes of 150–2,100m (500–6,900ft). Flower
clusters: *c.* 25mm (1in) across. Flower: *c.* 3mm ($\frac{1}{8}$in) across.

L. grandis *(L. mollis)*   **Plate 7** (45)
A very similar but much more common and widespread species and more
densely covered with short, soft hairs than *L. urticifolia* above. It prefers
wetter and colder conditions and is especially noticeable in the Machakos
district. Flower: *c.* 3mm ($\frac{1}{8}$in) across.

L. masaiensis *(L. venulosa)* is common in black cotton soils, especially near
Nairobi. It has many trailing or climbing stems and obovate to elliptic leaves
and is covered in coarse strong hairs. The white flowers are in loose or dense
clusters. Altitude range 1,300–3,000m (4,250–9,800ft). Flower: *c.* 2mm
($\frac{1}{16}$in) across.

111

Nepeta azurea   **Plate 42** (270)
An erect, down-covered perennial with lanceolate, cordate leaves and a terminal, spike-like inflorescence of purple-blue flowers. It often grows on the edges of forest and along the grassy banks of roads making an arresting sight when in full flower. It is found in areas of medium to heavy rainfall at altitudes of 1,800–3,600m (5,900–11,800ft) on Mt Elgon, the Cheranganis, the Mau, Aberdares, Mt Kenya and the Kisii Hills. Inflorescence: *c*. 2cm ($\frac{3}{4}$in) across.

Plectranthus barbatus   **Plate 47** (301)
An erect, soft, downy shrub which is also sometimes tree-like, one of more than 32 species of *Plectranthus* recorded in Kenya. It has ovate to ovate-elliptic, fleshy leaves and terminal racemes of large, bright blue flowers. It is an occasional plant in upland bushland and is often used by the Kikuyu people as a quick-growing hedge plant. Flower: *c*. 2cm ($\frac{3}{4}$in) long.

P. caninus is a low fleshy plant with ascending stems which bear elliptic to cuneate leaves and dense uninterrupted, terminal, spike-like racemes of bright blue or violet flowers, with apiculate bracts which are longer than the flowers. It has a strong and unpleasant smell and is widespread over much of Kenya in disturbed, dry, rocky country at altitudes 1,520–2,300m (5,000–7,500ft). Flower: *c*. 12mm ($\frac{1}{2}$in) long.

Plectranthus cylindraceus   **Plate 42** (268)
A down-covered, fleshy, scrambling shrub with elliptic to obovate leaves and sparsely-branched, densely-haired, spike-like racemes of small, powder blue flowers. It is locally common in dry rocky bushland in Kitale, Baringo, Rift Valley, Nanyuki, Voi, Machakos, Nairobi and Kajiado at altitudes of 610–2,070m (2,000–6,600ft). Inflorescence: *c*. 1cm ($\frac{3}{8}$in) across.

Plectranthus sylvestris   **Plate 44** (281)
A hairless, erect, sparsely-branched herb with ovate, acuminate leaves and bright blue flowers with white spots on the upper lip which are grouped in inflorescences that are usually branched. It is common in disturbed ground at the higher levels of montane forest, especially where there is bamboo, at altitudes of 2,300–2,750m (7,500–9,000ft) on Mt Elgon, Tinderet, Mau, the Aberdares and Mt Kenya. Flower: corolla *c*. 1cm ($\frac{3}{8}$in) long.

Salvia coccinea var. **coccinea**   **Plate 29** (188)
An erect annual with ovate, cordate leaves and conspicuous red flowers. It is an escape from gardens but is now found growing wild in disturbed places in the Nairobi and Mt Elgon areas from 1,600–1,800m (5,250–5,900ft). It was originally a native of America. Flower: *c*. 15mm ($\frac{5}{8}$in) across.

Salvia coccinea var. **lactea**   **Plate 4** (22)
A white variety of the same species as the preceding plant. It is also sometimes found in the wild as an escape from cultivations.

Salvia merjamie   **Plate 45** (293)
An erect, loosely hairy perennial which springs from a rosette of leaves and a thick, woody taproot. Its leaves are oblong and often lobed. Its pale purple flowers form dense racemes. It is locally common in grassland at 2,440–4,130m (8,000–13,500ft), especially where burning is a common practise. Flower: *c*. 1cm ($\frac{3}{8}$in) long.

S. nilotica, the commonest *Salvia* at 1,830–3,690m (6,000–12,100ft) is widespread at these altitudes. It is a hairy rhizomatous herb or plant with white, pink or purple flowers in branching and open racemes. Its leaves are opposite on the stem, pinnatifid and obovate with a hairy texture. Flower: corolla *c*. 1cm ($\frac{3}{8}$in) long.

Satureia biflora   **Plate 32** (207)
An erect, woody herb with elliptic to orbicular, entire leaves and axillary clusters of two to twenty pink flowers. It is a widespread and common species in upland dry grassland. The species includes an alpine form with the lower calyx teeth twice as long as the upper, which was formally classified as *S. biflora* and the lowland form formerly known as *S. punctata*, but they have been classified now as one. Altitude range 1,800–3,350m (6,000–11,000ft). Flower: *c*. 7mm ($\frac{1}{4}$in) long.

Satureia pseudosimensis   **Plate 36** (229)
A hairy shrub with weakly branching, ascending stems from a woody base. Its leaves are ovate to rounded and almost stalkless. Its purple or purplish-pink flowers form dense axillary clusters. It is common in clearings and at forest edges, mostly in the upper limits of montane forest and within the heath zone at altitudes of 1,700–3,500m (5,600–11,500ft). Flower: *c*. 1cm ($\frac{3}{8}$in) long.

61. COMMELINACEAE

A moderately-sized family of mainly tropical herbs. Their leaves are alternate with sheathing bases. There are three sepals, which may be free or united, and three delicate and deliquescent petals, one often smaller than the other two, which last only one day. Their six stamens may be reduced to staminodes. They have a superior, two- to three-locular ovary and the fruit is usually a compartmented capsule. There are 60 species in Kenya belonging to nine genera.

113

Aneilema acquinoctiale is a herb with trailing stems with hooked hairs and large yellow flowers. It is found in forests, forest edges and occasionally along roadsides, from 600–1,800m (2,000–6,000ft). Recorded in the Aberdares, Mt Kenya, Nyambeni Hills, Embu, Machakos, Nairobi and Kajiado. Flower: *c.* 23mm (*c.* 1in) across.

A. hockii is a herb with tufted ascending decumbent stems with hooked hairs and large mauve to blue flowers, in shape rather like a small pansy, carried in pairs, (sometimes in threes) opposite to each other on a long thin peduncle. It is common in grassland but also occurs in bushland and on rocky hills at lower altitudes and is recorded in the Aberdares, Narok, Magadi, Embu, Machakos, Nairobi and Kajiado, at 500–1,700m (1,600–5,600ft). Flower: *c.* 16mm ($\frac{5}{8}$in) across.

Anthericopsis sepalosa   Plate 40 (255)
A small herb with a basal rosette of leaves and large flowers. The flowers are occasionally white but usually either a very pale blue or tinged with blue. It has underground root tubers, and like other Commelinaceae, comes up quickly after rain and affords useful grazing before the grasses are available. It occurs in grassland at altitudes of 15–1,620m (50–5,300ft) and sometimes in woodland in Embu, Machakos and Kajiado at medium altitudes. It is also common in dry bushland such as the Northern Frontier district and the Tsavo National Parks. Flower: petals *c.* 25mm (1in) long.

Commelina forskalei   Plate 46 (300)
A small, trailing herb which roots at the nodes. Its very narrow leaves usually have undulate margins and its flowers are blue. It is a plant of grassland and bushland, most common below 910m (3,000ft) and recorded in Nyambeni, Baringo, Machakos and western Kenya from 10–1,650m (33–5,400ft). More than 20 species of *Commelina* are recorded in Kenya. Flower: *c.* 12mm (*c.* $\frac{1}{2}$in) across. *N.B.* All flower sizes in *Commelina* are approximate only.

C. benghalensis has bright blue flowers and a climbing or erect habit. It thrives in the damper areas of cultivated or disturbed patches of land over a wide area of Kenya and has a wide altitude tolerance, from 10–2,200m (33–7,200ft). It can often be seen growing strongly where cut off drains from roads keep the earth damp. Flower: *c.* 15mm ($\frac{5}{8}$in) across.

C. latifolia has darker blue flowers than *C. benghalensis* and broader, stronger leaves. It is also common in cultivated or disturbed ground and where cut off drains keep the ground moist, from 1–2,400m (3–7,900ft). Flower: *c.* 17mm (*c.* $\frac{5}{8}$in) across.

Commelina sp. A   Plate 47 (307)
An erect herb with dark blue flowers and hairy leaves and spathes (large

114

bracts). It occurs in seasonally swampy grassland. It is very common along the Thika-Nairobi road and has been recorded in the Aberdares, Mt Kenya, Magadi and Machakos areas from 1,070–2,290m (3,500–7,500ft). Flower: *c.* 15mm (⅝in) across.

Cyanotis barbata   Plate 32 (201)

An erect-stemmed, common annual which springs from small bulbs or rhizomes, with a spherical flower cluster at the end of the stem. The flowers of all seven species of *Cyanotis* recorded in Kenya are usually blue and white or pink. The specimen illustrated is a rare white-mauve form. It is characteristic of all species to have some long hairs on the filaments. This flower is usually found in grassland, sometimes in shallow soil over rocks, at medium altitudes 1,650–3,200m (5,400–10,500ft) in districts ranging from Mt Elgon and the Cheranganis to Kitui, Mumias and Kisii. Flower: *c.* 6mm (¼in) across.

C. foecunda is also a common annual or short-lived perennial but its flowers are much smaller than in *C. barbata.* They are white tinged with pink and occur on the nodes up the stem, which are weaker and less strongly erect than in *C. barbata.* It is found usually growing among rocks in grassland, bushland or forest edges in most of upland Kenya at altitudes from 900–2,300m (3,000–7,500ft). Flower: *c.* 4mm (*c.* ⅛in) across.

Murdannia simplex   Plate 43 (274)

A hairless herb with erect and ascending stems and lavender to bluish-mauve flowers. It is found in swamps, grassland, rocky places and almost everywhere except really dry areas at altitudes of 14–2,100m (45–6,900ft) and tends to flower in the afternoon. Flower: *c.* 15mm (⅝in) across.

M. clarkeana has bluish-mauve flowers and is found in temporarily waterlogged land on thin soil over rocks in grassland at 1,600–1,770m (5,250–5,800ft). It is common around Nairobi but rare elsewhere. Flower: *c.* 12mm (½in) across.

M. semiteres is a much smaller herb than *M. simplex.* It has tufted erect stems and tiny, blue to mauve flowers. It grows at the edge of temporary pools in rocky formations at 1,520–1,820m (5,000–6,000ft) but is confined to western Kenya and even there is rare. Flower: *c.* 6mm (¼in) across.

62. LILIACEAE

The Lily Family

A large, cosmopolitan family of perennial herbs or, less often, of woody climbers. Their flowers are usually regular and mostly in racemes with the perianth in two similar petaloid whorls of three and nearly always six

LILIACEAE

stamens, usually free. The ovary is superior and three-locular, the style usually single, occasionally threefold and the fruit a capsule or, less often, a berry. In classifying the *Liliaceae* the underground storage organs are important. Some genera such as *Ornithogalum* and *Scilla* have bulbs, others, such as *Bulbine*, have corms, while others, including *Anthericum* and *Chlorophytum* have swollen roots. There are some 100 species known in Kenya belonging to 20 genera.

Albuca wakefieldii is a robust plant up to 1m (3¼ft) or more tall, from an ovoid bulb produced into a neck which is sometimes fibrous; the leaves are variable, folded and often twisted with ciliated margins; often undulate in smaller forms of the plant. The flowers are bell-shaped, never opening fully, rather widely spaced on the peduncle and yellowish-green in colour with a darkish stripe down the middle of each perianth segment and the margins paler (yellowish). This is the commonest *Albuca* throughout Kenya, from 10–2,500m (30–8,200ft). It is a very variable species. Flower: *c.* 16mm ($\frac{5}{8}$in) across.

Aloe graminicola   **Plate 27** (175)
A small aloe with a rosette of triangular leaves with serrate edges. The orange-red flowers are borne on a branching head rounded in shape at the end of a long stem. It is often common in dry sandy grassland in northeast Kenya, especially around Naro Moru. Elephants are fond of aloes and can be observed eating them with relish. Where the aloes grow in abundance it is an indication that the elephant has been driven away or shot out for a time. Inflorescence: 25–30cm (10–12in).

A. amudatensis has a rosette of white-spotted, triangular leaves and solitary heads of pink to coral flowers on long peduncles. It is very similar to *A. graminicola* but it is uncommon and appears to be confined to northern areas above 910m (3,000ft). Inflorescence: *c.* 55cm (*c.* 22in) tall.

A. lateritia has a simple panicle of green and orange or red flowers and a sessile rosette of white-spotted and streaked leaves. It is an upland woodland species found up to altitudes of 2,100m (7,000ft) and appears to intergrade with *A. graminicola*. Inflorescence: *c.* 110cm (43in) tall.

Aloe rabaiensis   **Plate 26** (163)
A thicket-forming aloe with dense shrub-like growth and dull-green, hardly-crowded leaves. Its bright orange-red flowers are grouped in four- to seven-branched terminal panicles. It is locally common in rocky ground in Nairobi, Tinderet, Aberdares, Rift Valley, Machakos and Kajiado at altitudes 90–1,890m (3,000–6,200ft). Inflorescence: *c.* 60cm (*c.* 24in) tall.

Aloe secundiflora   **Plate 27** (172)
A large, fleshy herb with a rosette of green, unspotted, more or less glossy
leaves at ground level and a much-branched panicle of red flowers. All, or
nearly all the flowers are turned to one side of the inflorescence branch on
which they are borne. It is a common aloe, growing in several types of soil and
often among rocks, especially where elephant pressure was or is high. It is
found in fairly dry areas in Kitale, Baringo, Rift Valley, Magadi, Nanyuki,
and Kajiado districts at 700–1,800m (2,300–5,900ft) but does not occur in
very dry areas. Flowers: *c*. 35mm (1$\frac{3}{8}$in) long. Inflorescence: 100cm (3$\frac{1}{4}$ft) tall.

Aloe volkensii   **Plate 27** (171)
A tall, single-stemmed or, occasionally, branched tree growing up to 6m
(19ft) high. It has dull, grey-green leaves in a terminal rosette and much-
branched panicles of red flowers. It is common in rocky bushland in Narok
and Kajiado districts. Aloes sometimes vary considerably from place to
place, sometimes as a result of hybridization and, therefore, present even
experienced botanists with difficulties in identification. Altitude range
900–2,300m (3,000–7,500ft). Flower: perianth segments 35mm (1$\frac{3}{8}$in) long.
Inflorescence: 80cm (*c*. 32in) tall.

Bulbine abyssinica   **Plate 13** (85)
An erect plant which grows from a vertical rhizome with many fleshy roots.
The leaves spring upwards from a rosette at the base. Tufts of long yellow
hairs on the filaments make its bright yellow or sulphur yellow flowers look
puffy. It is a widespread lily of the grassland areas, common to many districts
and generally found above 1,220m (4,000ft). Flower: *c*. 8mm ($\frac{3}{8}$in) across.

Chlorophytum tenuifolium   **Plate 3** (14)
The *Chlorophytum* are herbaceous perennials with persistent or ephemeral
aerial shoots and creeping or erect rhizomes. The genus always has swollen
roots or root tubers and leaves are almost always in a basal rosette. All
Chlorophytum flowers are white or creamy-yellow in colour with a very fine
or broad greenish-brown stripe. This is a fairly large plant with a densely
fibrous rhizome and delicate, lanceolate, half-folded leaves in a rosette
ascending from the base. Its white flowers are usually solitary, alsi, rarely, in
pairs. It is locally common in black cotton soils and seasonally wet
grasslands, generally at altitudes of 100–1,650m (300–6,400ft). Flower: *c*.
28mm (1$\frac{1}{8}$in) across.

C. blepharophyllum has broad and long leaves, the lower ends of which tightly
clasp the flower stalk. The flowers, borne on one to three short branches,
and close together, are white in colour with a greenish-brown stripe on the
perianth. It is locally common in burnt grassland, especially in Mt Elgon area,
but is widespread from there to Mumias, Narok, Baringo, Kitale and the
Cheranganis. Inflorescence: 8–10cm (3–4in) long. Perianth segment: 7mm
(*c*. $\frac{1}{4}$in) long.

C. gallabatense grows from a short, compact rhizome with many long narrow roots which bear widely-spaced, small tubers. Its flowers are greenish-white and grow in a crowded raceme on loose branches up the stalk. In the afternoons they tend to be fully reflexed. It is a fairly frequent plant in grasslands, open woodlands and shallow soils, appearing after the first showers of rain in the higher Elgon, Mau and Aberdares areas on or above the 2,130m (7,000ft) contour, and in the Kitale, Kisii, Baringo, Nanyuki and Machakos districts. Inflorescence: 12–16cm ($4\frac{1}{4}$–6in) long. Perianth segment: 5mm ($\frac{1}{5}$in) long.

C. macrophyllum is a handsome plant which grows from a vertical or horizontal rhizome with many thick fleshy roots which carry ovoid tubers. It has broad slightly thick hairless leaves which are broadly lanceolate, wavy and crisped at margins, narrowing above the base. The inflorescence is up to 30cm (12in) tall, the raceme dense, usually simple with white flowers up to 1.5cm ($\frac{3}{5}$in) across in fascicles up to five in number. The lower bracts are long, project beyond the flowers and dry off blackish in colour. It is found on black cotton soil in grassland or open bushland with flowers opening a few at a time in the Narok, Machakos and Kajiado districts. It is common in the Ngong and Athi plains areas near Nairobi. Altitude range *c.* 1,350–1,800m (*c.*4,400–6,000ft). Flower: 12mm ($\frac{1}{2}$in) long.

C. micranthum has small greenish-white flowers which grow from a small rhizome. It is commonly seen in burnt grassland in the Kitale district, flowering after the first showers of rain have fallen. Inflorescence: *c.* 12mm (*c.* $\frac{1}{2}$in) long. Perianth segment: *c.* 5mm ($\frac{1}{5}$in) long.

Dipcadi viride is a hairless plant from 10–60cm (4–24in) in height, with linear to linear-lanceolate shiny, flaccid and indistinctly veined leaves which are variable in size. The shiny scape is terete and sometimes arcuate at the base. The flowers are green with a yellowish or khaki tinge, and the tips of the outer segments are curved outwards. The capsule is oblong in outline and about 1cm ($\frac{2}{5}$in) long. It is a common but variable species often found in wetter areas of grasslands and in bushland in Kitale, Baringo, Rift Valley, Embu, Machakos and Nairobi from 1,200–2,000m (4,000–6,500ft). Flower: *c.* 14mm ($\frac{9}{16}$in) long.

Drimia altissima *(Urginea altissima)* An erect robust herb from a large ovoid bulb drawn into a neck which is often covered with cotton-wool-like remains of old leaf bases. The flowers are whitish; the perianth deciduous and the segments free or slightly united at the base with a green to purple-brown median stripe. It is a common plant of rocky and sandy soils below 2,400m (8,000ft) in Elgon, Tinderet, Aberdares, Kitale, Mumias, Kisii, Baringo and

118

Rift Valley. Inflorescence: 0.6–1.8m (2–6ft) tall; Perianth segments 6–9mm ($\frac{1}{4}$–$\frac{3}{8}$in) long.

Gloriosa superba *(G. simplex)* **Plate 29** (185)
A most spectacular flower which grows vigorously from a V-shaped tuber, seeds itself easily and has been known to climb up to 5m (16ft) in height in upland forest. The tips of the lanceolate leaves act as tendrils. The flower is generally brilliant red, with the perianth segments reflexed, but it is also often striped with yellow or yellow and green. It is widespread below an altitude of 2,530m (8,300ft) and is sometimes called 'The Flame Lily'. A particularly beautiful variant often grows at lower altitudes, pale yellow in colour with a mauve to purple stripe. The variant is fairly widespread in Tsavo West National Park and can also be found in the Samburu district. Flower: *c.* 75mm (3in) across.

G. minor is smaller than *G. superba*, being under 50cm (1$\frac{1}{2}$ft) tall, and has narrower leaves and perianth segments. It grows in low-lying dry areas.

Kniphophia thomsonii is similar to the Red Hot Poker of European gardens. An erect herb from a fibrous, sometimes branched irregular rhizome with leaves up to 100cm (39in) long and a dense to lax raceme. The flowers are elongate and trumpet shaped and range in colour from yellow to a flame red. It is found along streams and in marshy places in Elgon, Mau, Cheranganis, Tinderet, Aberdares, Kitale, Baringo and Rift Valley at 1,000–1,600m (3,300–5,250ft). There is a dry area form which has shorter racemes and distinctly keeled leaves, the apices of which are sometimes triangular in section. The wet area form is more robust with flat leaves. Flower: up to 3cm (1$\frac{1}{8}$in) long.

Ornithogalum donaldsonii *(Albuca donaldsonii)* **Plate 3** (21)
A robust plant growing up to 1m (3$\frac{1}{4}$ft) or more in height from a large bulb which is 8cm (3in) across. Its large flowers are white to cream, their outer segments having a green median stripe, and borne on long, erect to ascending pedicels. It is a frequent plant in grassland and bushland, especially along the Mombasa road near Ulu and in the Machakos district at 520–1,000m (1,700–3,250ft). Flower: perianth segment *c.* 15mm ($\frac{5}{8}$in) long.

O. gracillimum is a small graceful plant growing to 5–20cm (2–8in) in height from a small bulb which is up to 1cm ($\frac{2}{5}$in) across. It has a few small and loosely-arranged white flowers which appear after the first rain. It is found in grassland and shallow soils overlying rocks in the upland areas of Kenya at altitudes 1,800–2,700m (5,900–8,850ft). Flower: 3–7mm ($\frac{1}{8}$–$\frac{1}{4}$in) long.

O. longibracteatum is the common species of this genus around Nairobi. It has long, linear-lanceolate leaves with the lamina usually folded and clasping

119

at the base and the margins often inrolled on the upper half. Its young conical raceme is dense with bracts projecting beyond the buds, thus as the white flowers open they make the raceme become rather lax. Its perianth segments have a broad green median stripe and white margins. Flower: c. 15mm (c. $\frac{5}{8}$in) across. Perianth segment: 1cm ($\frac{3}{8}$in) long.

Scilla kirkii   Plate 42 (269)
A low-growing plant with ovate to sword-shaped leaves which springs from a large bulb. Its flowers, which are carried on an upright stalk, are generally blue or purple. This attractive lily grows seasonally in wet soils and appears after rains, mainly in the Magadi, Machakos, Nairobi and Kajiado areas, it is also common in most dry areas at altitudes 9–1,750m (30–5,750ft). Flower: c. 1cm ($\frac{3}{8}$in) long.

S. indica is very similar with blue, or sometimes purple, flowers, but is a less robust species than S. kirkii. It is widespread at higher altitudes. It is possible that both species will eventually be classed as one. Flower: c. 1cm ($\frac{3}{8}$in) long.

Trachyandra saltii   Plate 40 (253)
A grass-like plant with many thin, but fairly stout roots. Its thread-like to linear leaves gradually dilate into a tubular, membranous base. In Kenya its axillary inflorescence is in the form of a simple, many-flowered raceme with one bract per flower and single pedicels. The single flowers usually open in the afternoon. They are white with a greenish to dark brown median stripe per segment. This is a very variable and adaptable species: three distinct forms have been recorded in Kenya. It is small in dry conditions, robust in wetter ones and found in Aberdares, Narok, Nanyuki, Machakos, Nairobi and Kajiado at altitudes of 880–2,130m (2,900–7,000ft). Flower: c. 11mm ($\frac{3}{8}$in) across.

63. AMARYLLIDACEAE
The Daffodil or Snowdrop Family

A medium-sized, widespread family of herbs. Their storage organ is a bulb, their leaves more or less linear rising from the bulb and their inflorescence an umbel subtended by bracts and borne on a leafless stalk springing from the bulb, or rarely, a solitary flower. They have a perianth of six petaloid segments, free or united into a tube below, often with a corona. There are six stamens and an inferior, three-locular ovary. Their fruit is a capsule or berry. There are 13 species in Kenya belonging to seven genera.

Ammocharis tinneana   Plate 35 (223)
A bulbous herb with a spreading fan of thick leaves around the base. The

inflorescence consists of about 20 long-tubed flowers opening out at their ends from a common peduncle and ranging in colour from pink to red. It is locally common in dry bushland or wooded grassland and can be found in Narok, Baringo, Magadi, Lower Embu and Kajiado districts at 640–1,800m (2,100–5,900ft). Flower: perianth tube 6–10cm ($2\frac{1}{4}$–4in) long.

A. angolensis *(A. heterostyla)* is a similar plant. It has fewer flowers, which are pink, not red, and is found in rocky bushland in western Kenya. Flower: perianth tube 4–8cm ($1\frac{1}{2}$–3in) long.

Boöphne disticha   Plate 30 (192)
A herb with a large bulb which annually produces a fan of leaves and a dense umbel of dull red flowers. Their pedicels lengthen and spread when in fruit to become stiff and straight so that the entire fruiting inflorescence can break away and roll over the ground, distributing the seeds in the process. The bulb is poisonous to cattle and the name comes from the Greek for 'ox-killer'. It is a good example of a so-called 'tumble-weed' and is locally common in rocky grassland at 1,520–2,440m (5,000–8,000ft) in Mt Elgon, Cheranganis, Tinderet, Narok, Baringo, Rift Valley, Nairobi and Kajiado districts. Flower: perianth *c*. 3cm ($1\frac{1}{8}$in) long.

Crinum macowanii   Plate 33 (210)
A large, bulbous plant with thick, heavy, dull grey-green leaves which spring out from the ground. Its long, tubular flowers are white with pink stripes, earning it the popular name of 'Pyjama Lily'. It is fairly common in many districts in open grassland and along roadside verges at altitudes of 1,500–2,300m (4,900–7,500ft). Three other species are found in Kenya at lower altitudes. *C. kirkii* is a name wrongly applied to *C. macowanii* in the past: it is a southern species not found in Kenya. Flower: perianth lobes *c*. 3cm ($1\frac{1}{8}$in) long; perianth tube *c*. 10cm (4in) long.

Cyrtanthus sanguineus subsp. **ballyi**   Plate 28 (177)
An erect herb with linear strap-shaped leaves and a funnel-shaped, bright red perianth with one to three flowers together. It is locally common in stony grasslands and sometimes makes a good display in the Nairobi Game Park but, although no exact record can be made, there are probably not more than 3,000 plants in Kenya. It is, therefore, an endangered species and should on no account be disturbed or collected from its habitat. Flower: perianth 5–10cm (2–4in) long.

C. sanguineus subsp. **salmonoides** resembles subsp. *ballyi* but has solitary, or occasionally two, pink to orange flowers. It has been found near the Ngong Hills, up to 1,950m (6,500ft) altitude and in the Kajiado district. Flower: perianth 7–9cm ($2\frac{3}{4}$–$3\frac{1}{2}$in) long.

Scadoxus multiflorus *(Haemanthus multiflorus)*　　　　**Plate 29** (182)
The magnificent red flowers of this lily appear with the first rains and before its thick, upright leaves show themselves. They are carried on a single long, thin stem, as many as 150 making up a single head, and become pinkish as they fade, giving the appearance of a gigantic shaving brush. It is widespread in rocky places, riverine forest and open grassland and often found growing in the shade of trees or on the edges of large ant heaps at altitudes up to 2,150m (6,750ft). It is popularly called the Fire Ball Lily.

A slightly different form, which prefers a more arid habitat can be seen on Mt Marsabit in the forest zone, carpeting the ground for hundreds of square metres. The individual flowers are slightly more widely spaced and redder than in the other form and do not present such a strong impression of a shaving brush. The bulbs of both forms are often very deeply placed in the soil. Inflorescence: 14–19cm ($5\frac{1}{2}$–$7\frac{1}{2}$in) across.

64. IRIDACEAE

The Iris Family

A medium-sized, mainly temperate family of herbs, most numerous in South Africa and South America. Their rootstock is a corm, rhizome or, rarely, a bulb, and their leaves are narrowly linear, basal or on the stem. The regular or zygomorphic flowers have a petaloid perianth and are often tubular below with six segments. There are three stamens and an inferior ovary. The fruit is a capsule. There are 18 species recorded in Kenya belonging to ten genera but they are rarely found below 1,000m (3,300ft) altitudes.

Aristea alata is an erect, tufted herb with numerous fans of short, stiff leaves at the base and an erect, branching inflorescence of clusters of blue flowers; the stem is flattened with narrow wings. It is locally common in highland wet grassland from 1,700–3,700m (5,600–12,100ft) in Elgon, Cheranganis, Tinderet, Mau, Aberdares, Kitale and Kisii. Flower: *c.* 9mm ($\frac{3}{8}$in) across.

A. angolensis is an erect herb with rather few very long leaves at base, bearing an erect, leafy stem with sessile clusters of blue flowers; the stem is flattened but not winged. It also does not have the numerous fans of short stiff leaves at the base as in *A. alata*. It is locally common in wet grassland in Western Kenya, Elgon, Tinderet, the Aberdares and Kitale from 1,700–2,500m (5,600–8,200ft). Flower: *c.* 13mm ($\frac{1}{2}$in) across.

Dierama pendulum is a robust, densely-tufted perennial, growing from a rhizomatous rootstock with laterally flattened linear leaves and branched panicles of delicate, nodding and short tubular pinkish-purple flowers. It is common in high altitude grassland from 2,400–3,900m (7,900–12,800ft). Flower: *c.* 25mm (1in) across.

Gladiolus natalensis   **Plate 25** (157)

One of the ancestors of the cultivated garden gladiolus, this is similar to the *G. primulinus* garden varieties which have been evolved by plant breeders. Its flowers are borne on a long, erect stem and are markedly hooded. They range from yellowish-brown to orange in colour and are often streaked or flecked with brown. It is a common plant in grassland from 1,200–3,050m (4,000–10,000ft) but rarely found above that higher altitude. A local species, *G. species 'A'*, with yellow flowers streaked with orange, is found in rocky, wooded grassland in western Kenya. Flower: *c.* 2cm ($\frac{3}{4}$in) across.

Gladiolus ukambanensis *(Acidanthera candida, A. ukambanensis)* **Plate 2** (8)

An erect herb springing from a round corm with a fibrous covering. Its long white flowers are beautifully scented and have a tube 10cm (4in) long. It flowers copiously in years of good rainfall but is capricious in its flowering, in some years being abundant and in others only sparing. It is found in stony grasslands in the Machakos district at altitudes of 610–2,100m (2,000–7,000ft) but it is not common. Flower: *c.* 35mm ($1\frac{3}{8}$in) across.

Gladiolus watsonioides   **Plate 29** (183)

The finest of the Kenyan gladioli. Its flowers are bright red with a curved perianth tube 30–40mm (*c.* $1\frac{1}{2}$in) long. It grows only at high altitudes in stony soils of the alpine and subalpine regions from 3,050m (10,000ft) and higher, on the Aberdares and Mt Kenya. Flower: *c.* 25mm (1in) across.

Romulea fischeri   **Plate 38** (240)

A member of the Iris family with single, star-like, mauve or pale purple flowers. It grows in wet upland and alpine stony grassland in all the higher altitude areas above 1,830m (6,000ft) in Elgon, the eastern Cheranganis and eastern Tinderet and above 2,130m (7,000ft) in western Cheranganis, western Tinderet, the Plateau, Mau, Aberdares, Loita Hills and northern and western slopes of Mt Kenya. On the south and east slopes of Mt Kenya it is found from 1,520m (5,000ft) upwards. Flower: *c.* 22mm ($\frac{7}{8}$in) across.

R. keniensis is similar to *R. fischeri* in appearance but has smaller flowers and grows in stony wet soils, especially alongside streams, in the alpine zones of Mt Kenya and the Aberdares. Flower: perianth *c.* 25mm (1in) long.

65. HYPOXIDACEAE

A small family of perennial herbs found mainly in the Southern Hemisphere. Their rootstock is in the form of a fibrous rhizome or corm and their leaves are basal, sheathing below. Their star-like perianth has six segments, usually six stamens and an inferior ovary. They are found at all altitudes up to

3,050m (10,000ft) but never in really dry areas. Six species are recorded in Kenya, all belonging to the same genus.

Hypoxis obtusa   Plate 21 (133)
A perennial plant which grows from a corm and has narrow, strap-like, recurved leaves. Its yellow flowers are held upright and open on a long thin stalk or scape. It is common in burnt grassland and the moister parts of shallow soils at altitudes of 910–2,100m (3,000–7,000ft) throughout Kenya, except possibly in the West. Flower: c. 15mm ($\frac{5}{8}$in) across.

H. villosa is similar to *H. obtusa* but has smaller flowers. It is found in much the same districts and occasionally in black cotton soils, especially near Nairobi. Flower: perianth 11mm ($\frac{3}{8}$in) long.

H. multiflora has dense or loose racemes of large yellow flowers which tend to centre themselves in the middle of upright or semi-erect, broad, linear-lanceolate leaves which spring from a largish corm. It is locally common in burnt grassland in Kitale, Elgon and the Cheranganis.

66. ORCHIDACEAE
The Orchid Family

A very large family, mainly of epiphytic and tropical plants but also with numerous terrestrial species, many of which are temperate. They are almost absent from dry tropical areas. They are herbs with rhizomes, root tubes or leaves swollen at the base to form pseudo-bulbs. Their flowers are zygomorphic, the perianth having two whorls of three, the outer either sepaloid or petaloid, the inner petaloid. The middle petal differs from the other two and forms a lip. Often either the lip or the dorsal is spurred. There are one or two stamens united with the style to form the 'column'. Pollen becomes stuck together in waxy masses called pollinia. The ovary is inferior, and the fruit is a capsule containing innumerable minute seeds. There are about 220 species found in Kenya belonging to 38 genera.

Ansellia gigantea var. nilotica   Plate 22 (137)
Commonly called the Leopard Orchid, this is a robust giant, the height of which varies from 1–2m (3–6ft). Its inflorescence is usually, but not always, branching, with yellow flowers spotted with brown. It is epiphytic in habit and found on rocks or amongst roots and branches, usually in sunny positions or light shade. It is common at the coast on palm trees and found in nearly all the medium to wetter rainfall districts up to an altitude of 2,130m (7,000ft). Flower: c. 32mm ($1\frac{1}{4}$in) across.

ORCHIDACEAE

Bonatea steudneri   Plate 2 (8)
A robust herb which grows to 25–125cm (10–50in) in height bearing 10–20 leaves and 6–30 green and white flowers. Its bracts are leafy, shorter than the pedicel with ovary; the lip claw is 15–30mm ($\frac{5}{8}$–1$\frac{1}{5}$in) long then divides, the middle lobe is linear and usually bent sharply backwards from the middle, the side lobes much longer, 15–85mm (1–3$\frac{3}{8}$in), and the spur usually 1–2cm ($\frac{2}{5}$–$\frac{3}{4}$in) long and usually twisted. It is found in bush, scrub and grassland at the edge of thickets, by roadsides and in rocky places at 1,520–2,400m (5,000–8,000ft) altitudes and is widespread in Kenya.

Diaphananthe fragrantissima   Plate 6 (36)
An epiphytic plant with a woody stem which attaches itself to the branches of tall trees. The flowers are whitish-green and attached to the leafless stem in groups of two to four individual flowers. It grows within the forest zone at altitudes of 1,070–1,500m (3,500–5,000ft). Flower: *c.* 15mm ($\frac{5}{8}$in) across; spur, 7mm (*c.* $\frac{1}{4}$in) long.

D. pulchella is similar to *D. fragrantissima* but with longer flowers which are semi-transparent, a darker green and arranged in groups of six to eight. It is found in dry forests at altitudes of 1,350–2,100m (4,500–7,000ft) on Mt Elgon and in the Aberdares and Machakos districts. Flower: *c.* 12mm (*c.* $\frac{1}{2}$in) across; spur, *c.* 10mm ($\frac{3}{8}$in) long.

D. rutilla is often insecurely attached to its host tree by short aerial roots with larger roots hanging free. Its leaves are rather leathery and touched with purple. Its dingy, greenish-purple flowers are densely arranged. It is widespread in forested areas at altitudes of 200–2,100m (700–7,000ft) in the Mau, Aberdares, Mt Kenya, Mumias, Kisii, Machakos and Nairobi areas. Flower: 4mm ($\frac{3}{16}$in) across; spur, *c.* 6mm ($\frac{1}{4}$in) long.

Disa erubescens has flowering stems from 30–90cm (12–36in) high with bracts shorter than the very distinctive large orange, red or deep scarlet flowers. The dorsal sepal is slightly incurved but not really hooded and spurred at about the middle. The spur projects backwards or slightly upwards, and the petals are bi-lobed with the lip narrowly linear and 1mm (less than $\frac{1}{16}$in) broad. It is found in short upland grassland, particularly where drainage is poor and in swamps from 1,400–2,600m (4,500–8,500ft) in Elgon, the Cheranganis, Tinderet, Mau, Kitale and Kisii. Flower: *c.* 18cm (*c.* $\frac{3}{4}$in) across.

D. hircicornis has a flowering stem from 30–85cm (12–33in) in height, with dense inflorescence; 16 to many flowered; the lowermost bracts often overtopping the pale pink to purple flowers. The dorsal sepal is curved forward and narrowly conical and in turn narrows into a short slender spur which is usually curved round like the horn of a goat. The petals are entire and erect with a linear-spathulate lip. It is found in wet grassland and swamps, often near streams from 1,500–2,600m (5,000–8,500ft) in the Cheranganis, Tinderet and Kitale. Flower: *c.* 12mm ($\frac{1}{2}$in) across.

D. scutellifera has flowering stems 25–75cm (10–30in) high. The inflorescence is densely, many flowered; the lowermost bracts overtopping the pink flowers; dorsal sepal erect, convex and spurred below the middle. The petals are erect and bi-lobed, in the upper part with the lip pendent and linear. It is found in damp grassland and grassy rocky slopes from 1,800–2,400m (6,000–8,000ft) in Elgon, Tinderet, Mau, Aberdares, and Mt Kenya. Flower: *c.* 10mm ($\frac{3}{8}$in) across.

D. stairsii is a terrestial or, rarely, epiphytic herb with slender hairy roots but no tubers; the inflorescence is often cylindrical rather than dense; the lower bracts longer than the pink to wine-red flowers with the dorsal sepal erect, convex and hooded with a pendent spur below the middle. The petals are entire with a ligulate lip 2–3mm ($\frac{1}{8}$in) broad. It is always found above 2,700m (9,000ft) in grassland, moorland and rocky areas and recorded in Elgon, the Cheranganis, Aberdares and Mt Kenya. Flower: *c.* 120mm (4$\frac{3}{4}$in) across.

Eulophia horsfallii *(E. porphyroglossa)* **Plate 38** (245)
A robust orchid growing from a subterranean rhizome with leaves plicate to a height of 1m (3$\frac{1}{4}$ft) and a width of 15cm (6in), the peduncle rising to three to ten feet. Its flowers are large, the bronze-purple sepals reflexed, the petals longer than broad and mauve, often white on the inner surface. The lip is distinctly three-lobed, with several rows of tall lamellae on the middle lobe. It grows in swamps and at river edges up to altitudes of 2,400m (8,000ft), mainly in northwest, western and central Kenya. Flower: *c.* 4cm (1$\frac{1}{2}$in) across.

Eulophia stenophylla **Plate 22** (138)
A herb with ovoid pseudobulbs at or above ground level. Its leaves are usually less than 2cm ($\frac{3}{4}$in) wide and are well developed at the time of flowering. The flowers have yellow petals with a grey inner surface, the lip yellow with purplish veins, and the sepals are green overlaid with brown. It is usually found in bush or among rocks with some shade at altitudes of 610–1,830m (2,000–6,000ft) and is recorded in Nairobi, Narok and the Rift Valley near Nakaru. Flower: not more than 25mm (1in) in diameter.

Microcoelia guyoniana is a small to robust plant with thicker roots and white flowers larger than *M. smithii*. The perianth parts are wider and the anther cap yellow or brown. The spur is conical with the apex yellowish, greenish or brownish. It is found in dry forest and bush from 1,500–2,000m (5,000–6,500ft) in Kitale, Western Kenya, Kisii, Narok, Baringo, Rift Valley and Nairobi. Flower: *c.* 4mm ($\frac{3}{16}$in) across. This genus has no leaves, photosynthesis taking place in the roots.

M. smithii is a tiny, almost minute, plant with very thin roots; the flowers are white with the spur about the same length as the lip and often tinged with green or pink at the tip; the perianth parts are often rather narrow. It is found in dry forest and bush from 300–1,800m (1,00–6,000ft) in coastal forests and in Nairobi. Flower: *c.* 3mm ($\frac{1}{8}$in) across.

Polystachya transvaalensis   Plate 10 (65)
An epiphyte with long and slender pseudobulbs which bears four to six elliptic, thickened leaves with rounded tips. Its inflorescence is paniculate with yellowish-green or reddish-green sepals and paler, spathulate petals with the lip nearly white and purple-spotted. It is found in highland forest in Kenya at altitudes of 1,520–3,050m (5,000–10,000ft). Flower: *c.* 15mm (*c.* $\frac{5}{8}$in) across.

Rangaeris amaniensis   Plate 4 (23)
An epiphyte with elongated and often branched stems which bear two rows of short, leathery leaves near the tip and have very thick, robust roots. Its inflorescence of whitish flowers is usually longer than the leaves. It is found in nearly all dry forest in Kenya at altitudes of 1,370–2,130m (4,500–7,000ft). Flower: *c.* 2cm ($\frac{3}{4}$in) across; spur, 12cm ($4\frac{3}{4}$in) long.

Satyrium cheirophorum has a flowering stem from 25–70cm (10–27in) in height, bearing six to ten leaves with the two or three near the base much larger than the others. The inflorescence is cylindrical with ten to many pale or bright pink flowers and slender spurs from 10–18mm ($\frac{3}{8}$–$\frac{3}{4}$in) long. It is found in damp or poorly drained upland grassland from 1,500–2,600m (5,000–8,500ft) in Mau, Aberdares, Kisii and Nairobi. Flower: *c.* 24mm (1in) across.

S. crassicaule has a flowering stem 30–120cm (12–48in) high with a tuft of broadly lanceolate leaves at the base and other smaller ones along the stem. The inflorescence is densely flowered with many pink to mauve but rarely white flowers with slender spurs, 8–13mm ($\frac{5}{16}$–$\frac{1}{2}$in) long. It is found in damp grassland or swamps especially by streams and often in running water from 1,700–3,040m (5,500–10,000ft) in Elgon, Tinderet, Mau, Aberdares, Mt Kenya, Kitale and Rift Valley. Flower *c.* 6mm ($\frac{1}{4}$in) across.

S. sacculatum has a flowering stem from 30–120cm (12–48in) in height, with 13 to 17 sheathing leaves, and a sterile shoot up to 7cm (2–3in) high bearing three to six leaves. The inflorescence is cylindrical and densely flowered; the flowers are many, orange-yellow to red (flame colour) and rarely white, with the margins of the petals ciliate. The spurs are 8.5–10.5mm (*c.* $\frac{5}{16}$–$\frac{7}{16}$in) long, usually with a pair of very short spurs in front. It is found in short grassland and amongst scattered bushes from 1,500–2,500m (5,000–8,300ft) in Elgon, Tinderet, Mau, Aberdares, Mt Kenya and Rift Valley. Flower: *c.* 15mm ($\frac{5}{8}$in) across.

S. schimperi has a flowering stem from 15–60cm (6–24in) in height, bearing five to seven leaves and a narrow cylindrical inflorescence of nine to many greenish or yellowish-green flowers with all petals with a papillose margin and the spurs slender and 5–8mm ($\frac{3}{16}$–$\frac{5}{16}$in) long. It is found in upland grassland often among rocks from 2,100–2,900m (7,000–9,500ft) in the Cheranganis, Tinderet, Mau and Aberdares. Flower: *c.* 10mm (*c.* $\frac{3}{8}$in) across.

63.   GRAMINEAE (Poaceae)

The Grass Family

A very large family of herbs, or much less often, trees or shrubs (bamboos) found all over the world. They are adapted to wind pollination and the flowers are, therefore, inconspicuous. The perianth is reduced to minute scales between the enclosing bracts. There are usually three stamens with loose, dangling anthers and the styles are usually two in number and feathery. The ovary is superior with one ovule and the fruit is a grain as in wheat. There are 555 species in Kenya belonging to 141 genera.

This is the largest Kenyan family except for the Leguminoseae, which has 592 species if its three subfamilies are considered as one.

The *Gramineae* are easily confused with the *Cyperaceae*, the Sedge family, which has 24 species in Kenya belonging to 18 genera. The stems of the *Cyperaceae* are usually solid and three-angled with the leaf sheath united to form a tube, while in the *Gramineae* the stems are cylindrical and hollow with the leaf sheath split down one side.

Cenchrus ciliaris   **Plate 2** (12)
This is a tall, showy grass which can reach a height of up to 130cm (4ft) and has feathery inflorescences. It is found at altitudes up to 1,700m (5,600ft) in dry grassland areas such as the Chalbi Desert. Inflorescence: *c.* 13mm ($\frac{1}{2}$in) across.

Conversion tables

Inches to Millimetres

1 inch = 25.400mm

$\frac{1}{8}$in =   3.175mm
$\frac{1}{4}$in =   6.350mm
$\frac{3}{8}$in =   9.525mm
$\frac{1}{2}$in = 12.700mm
$\frac{5}{8}$in = 15.875mm
$\frac{3}{4}$in = 19.050mm
$\frac{7}{8}$in = 22.225mm
1in = 25.400mm
2in = 50.800mm
3in = 76.200mm
4in = 101.600mm
5in = 127.000mm
10in = 254.000mm
12in = 304.800mm

Millimetres to Inches

1mm = 0.039370in

5mm = 0.197in
10mm = 0.394in
20mm = 0.787in
30mm = 1.181in
40mm = 1.575in
50mm = 1.969in
60mm = 2.362in
70mm = 2.756in
80mm = 3.150in
90mm = 3.543in
100mm = 3.937in

Inches to Centimetres

1in = 2.54cm

1in = 2.540cm
2in = 5.080cm
3in = 7.620cm
4in = 10.160cm
5in = 12.700cm
6in = 15.240cm
7in = 17.780cm
8in = 20.320cm
9in = 22.860cm
10in = 25.400cm
11in = 27.940cm
12in = 30.480cm

Centimetres to Inches

1cm = 0.393701in

1cm = 0.393701in
2cm = 0.787in
3cm = 1.181in
4cm = 1.575in
5cm = 1.969in
6cm = 2.362in
7cm = 2.756in
8cm = 3.150in
9cm = 3.543in
10cm = 3.937in
20cm = 7.874in
30cm = 11.811in
40cm = 15.748in
50cm = 19.685in
100cm = 39.370in

Feet to Metres	Metres to Feet
1ft = 0.3048m	*1m = 3.280840ft*
1ft = 0.3048m	1m = 3.280840ft
2ft = 0.610m	2m = 6.562ft
3ft = 0.914m	3m = 9.843ft
4ft = 1.219m	4m = 13.123ft
5ft = 1.524m	5m = 16.404ft
6ft = 1.829m	6m = 19.685ft
7ft = 2.134m	7m = 22.966ft
8ft = 2.438m	8m = 26.247ft
9ft = 2.743m	9m = 29.528ft
10ft = 3.048m	10m = 32.808ft
50ft = 15.240m	50m = 164.042ft
100ft = 30.480m	100m = 328.084ft
200ft = 60.960m	200m = 656.168ft
300ft = 91.440m	300m = 984.252ft
400ft = 121.920m	400m = 1,312.336ft
500ft = 152.400m	500m = 1,640.420ft
600ft = 182.880m	600m = 1,968.504ft
700ft = 213.360m	700m = 2,296.588ft
800ft = 243.840m	800m = 2,624.672ft
900ft = 274.320m	900m = 2,952.756ft
1,000ft = 304.800m	1,000m = 3,280.840ft

Glossary

This glossary explains common technical terms and other botanical expressions which it has been necessary to use in the text and others which the reader may encounter in extending his or her researches.

Achene Dry, single-seeded fruit with seed distinct from cell wall
Aculeate Armed with prickles or thorns
Acuminate Narrowed to tip so that sides are concave (see p. 22)
Acute Sharply pointed but not tapered (see p. 22)
Adaxial Nearest the axis
Alternate Neither opposite nor whorled, alternating along stem (see p. 18)
Amplexicaul Having a large base that circles the stem
Anther Part of the flower producing male pollen (see p. 16)
Annual Plant living one year or less, usually shallow rooted and never woody
Apiculate Ending in a short sharp point (see p. 23)
Appressed Pressed closely against but not joined to the surface
Arcuate Arched
Ascending Growing or sloping upwards
Awn Long bristle-like appendage
Axil The upper angle between stem and branch or leaf growing from it (see p. 18)
Axillary Rising from an axil

Biennial Plant living two years, often only flowering in the second year
Bifurcate Forked into two parts or branches
Bilabiate Divided into two lips, as when two or three lobes of a calyx or corolla stand separate from the others forming an upper and lower lip
Bipinnate When the pinnae of a pinnate leaf are themselves pinnate (see p. 19)
Bract Small leaf-like organ or modified leaf, especially one with a flower or inflorescence growing from its axil (see p. 17)
Bracteole Small, usually scale-like bract on or close to the calyx of a flower
Bulbil Small, bulb-like organ at base of leaves or in place of flowers which breaks off to form new plants

Caespitose Growing in dense tufts
Calyx Outer (usually green) protective envelope of a flower, consisting of free or united sepals (see p. 16)
Campanulate Bell-shaped
Canescent White or greyish due to the presence of numerous short white hairs
Capitate Gathered into a compact cluster or head
Capitulum Compact cluster of usually sessile flowers, as in many daisies
Carpel Female reproductive organ, consisting of ovary, style and stigma; carpels may be fused to form a single pistil
Caudate See Cuspidate
Chartaceous Papery

131

Composite Belonging to the Daisy family, *Compositae*

Compressed Flattened lengthwise, either side to side (laterally) or from front to back (dorsally)

Conical Cone-shaped

Contorted Twisted; used mainly of petals

Convolute Rolled lengthwise with margins or sides curling

Cordate Heart-shaped; with basal lobes rounded and a notch between (see p. 20)

Coriaceous Leathery

Corolla The petals as a whole, especially when joined (see p. 16)

Corona Crown-like circle of living appendages between corolla and stamens, as in *Passiflora* (The Passion fruit family)

Corymb Inflorescence or flower form in which branches or pedicels start from different points but reach approximately the same level giving a more or less flat top

Crenate Edged with rounded notches (see p. 22)

Crispate Curled or waved

Cuneate Wedge-shaped; cuneate leaves are attached at the narrow end (see p. 23)

Cuspidate Abruptly tipped with a sharp point (caudate) (see p. 23)

Cyclic Having the leaves or petals in whorls

Cyme Inflorescence in which the first flower to open is the terminal bud of the main stem and subsequent flowers develop as terminal buds of lateral stems (see p. 17)

Declinate Inclined downwards

Decumbent Lying flat with the tip growing upwards

Deflexed Bent downwards

Deliquescent Forming many branches. Also becoming pulpy when dying

Dentate Having a toothed edge (see p. 22)

Depressed Flattened, as though pressed from above

Descending Growing downwards

Dichotomous Branching by repeated division into equal parts

Dicotyledon Plant having two embryonic seed leaves and leaves with net-like veins

Diffuse Spreading loosely over a large area

Dioecious Unisexual, having male flowers on one plant and female on another.

Distal Furthest from the axis or point of attachment

Drupe Fleshy fruit with a stone enclosing the seed, as in cherry, peach, olive

Eglandular Without glands

Elliptic Shaped like an ellipse

Elongate Drawn out

Emarginate Having a notched tip or edge (see p. 23)

Endosperm Tissue within the seed of a flowering plant which nourishes the embryo and often surrounds it

Entire Having an uninterrupted margin or edge, without teeth or lobes

Epicalyx Ring of sepal-like bracts just below the true sepals

Epiphyte Plant growing on another plant but not deriving nourishment from it

Ephemeral Transitory, short-lived as with many annuals

Exstipulate Without stipules

Facultative Able to exist under more than one set of environmental conditions

Fascicle Cluster

-fid Divided into parts or lobes (as trifid, cleft into three parts)

Filament Stalk of a stamen
Filiform Threadlike
Fissile Tending to split
Flexuose Full of bends, zig-zag
Floret Small flower, especially one forming part of a larger head or cluster
  Disc floret: petals joined in a tube end in five short teeth
  Ray floret: petals joined in a tube end in conspicuous flat flap
Floriferous Bearing flowers
Flower The reproductive organs of a plant and the envelope which protects them (see
  p. 16)
Fluted With deep vertical channels
-foliate Bearing leaves
-foliolate Bearing leaflets (as tri-foliolate, having three leaflets)
Form A division of a species, and subordinate to a variety, having trivial differences
  (such as colour) from others in the species
Free Not united

Glabrous Hairless
Glandular Having glands
Glaucous Covered with a waxy or powdery bloom as on a plum or cabbage leaf. Dull
  grey green or blue green in colour.
Globose Spherical
Glutinous Sticky
Gymnosperm Plant bearing its seeds naked on the surface, often arranged on cones or
  below fern-like leaves
Gynoecium Carpels of a flowering plant

Habit General appearance and manner of growth
Hastate Having a pointed tip and two outward-pointing lobes at base (from the latin
  for spear, *hasta*)
Head Mass of sessile or subsessile flowers grouped on a common receptacle or support
Herbaceous Fleshy, not woody
Hirsute Covered with stiff bristle-like hairs

Imbricate Overlapping, especially of flower buds in which one sepal or petal is wholly
  internal and one wholly external, the others overlapping at the edge only
Incised Having sharply and deeply indented edges
Indehiscent Remaining closed when ripe
Indumentum Covering: of hair, scales, wax etc
Induplicate Bent or folded inwards with the edges touching but not overlapping
Inflorescence Flowering part of a plant and the arrangement of flowers upon it
Interpetiolar Between petioles
Involucral Like, or resembling, a ring of bracts
Involucre Whorl of bracts surrounding the base of a flower or flower cluster

Keel (1) Lower part of the flower of a member of the Pea family in which two petals
  combine to conceal the stamens and styles (see p. 16)
  (2) A projecting ridge

Laciniate Jagged or slashed and divided into long slender, irregular taper-pointed
  segments, or indentations like a fringe

Lamina Flat blade of a leaf or petal
Lanate With soft, entangled, woolly hairs
Lanceolate Spear-shaped, narrowly oval and pointed (see p. 20)
Lax Loose, not compact
Leaflet A single division of a compound leaf
Liane Woody climber
Ligulate Strap-shaped, provided with a strap-shaped appendage (especially used of ray florets of many *Compositae*)
Limb Main branch
Linear Long and very narrow, with almost parallel edges, such as grass leaves
Lobe Division of a leaf, perianth or anther. Lobed margins usually have large rounded teeth and shallow notches or sinuses
Lobulate Divided into little lobes
Locular Compartmented
Loculus Compartment

Mericarp Partial fruit, such as one of the halves of the fruit of an *Umbellifer*
Monocotyledon Plant with only one embryonic seed leaf and leaves with parallel veins and flowers with parts in threes
Mucronate Terminating in a sharp point (see p. 23)
Node Joint, point on a stem or branch at which a leaf or further branch is produced or borne

Oblanceolate Having a broad rounded apex and a tapering base
Oblique Slanting, unequal-sided
Oblong With sides more or less parallel and a rounded apex, two to six times as long as broad (see p. 21)
Obovate Shaped like the longitudinal section of an egg, with the narrower end at the base (see p. 20)
Obtuse Blunt or rounded at the tip (see p. 22)
Odd-pinnate Pinnate with an odd terminal leaf
Orbicular Flat with a circular outline
Ovate Shaped like the longitudinal section of an egg, with the broader end at the base (see p. 21)
Ovule Grain-like body containing the egg cell which, after fertilisation, develops into the seed

Palmate Having five lobes, like the outspread fingers of a hand
Panicle Compound raceme, a (usually) pyramidal inflorescence in which the axis is divided into several branches bearing flowers, the lower branches being longer and blossoming earlier than the upper branches
Papillose Covered with minute nipple-like protuberances
Pappus Tuft or ring of hairs or scales around the fruits of plants of the family *Compositae* which aids dispersal by the wind
Parasite Plant which grows on another plant and derives nourishment from it
Parietal Having ovules attached to the walls
Parted Not quite divided: used of simple leaves divided almost to the midrib or to the base of the blade
Pedicel Stalk bearing an individual flower of an inflorescence

GLOSSARY

Peduncle Common stalk of an inflorescence or the stalk of a single flower which is the only inflorescence of that plant
Pedunculate Having, or growing from, a peduncle
Pendulous Hanging down, suspended from above
Perennial Living for more than two years
Perianth Outer part of a flower, consisting of calyx or corolla or both; used when it is difficult to distinguish between calyx and corolla
Perigynous Having a concave or flat receptacle with distinct carpels surrounded by other floral parts
Persistent Remaining attached to the plant after the normal time of withering
Petaloid Petal-like
Petiole Stalk by which a leaf is attached to the plant
Petiolate Having a petiole or stalk
Petiolule Stalk of a leaflet
Phyllaries Bracts forming the cup or involucre
Pilose Covered with rather soft, long, slender scattered hairs
Pinna (pinnae) Primary division of a pinnate leaf
Pinnate Having leaflets growing opposite each other in pairs on either side of the stem
Pinnatifid Having the margin (of a leaf) divided into lobes reaching less than half way to the midrib
Pinnatilobed Having the margin (of a leaf) divided into lobes reaching more than or half way to the midrib
Pinnativeined Where, on an entire leaf, the veins are pinnate
Pistil Female reproductive part of a flower
Plicate Folded like a fan
Plumose Feathered; having fine hairs on each side
Precocious Flowering before the leaves open
Procumbent Lying along the surface of the ground
Prostrate Synonymous with procumbent
Proximal Nearest to the axis or point of attachment
Pubescent Covered with short soft hairs or down
Puberulous Minutely pubescent
Pustulate With slight pimple-like swellings
Pyriform Pear-shaped

Raceme Inflorescence in which the flowers are borne on pedicels or stalks along an unbranched axis or stem, the lower flowers opening first (see p. 17)
Racemose Having the characteristics of, or being like, a raceme
Rachis The axis of an inflorescence or of a compound leaf (see p. 19)
Ranked Arranged in rows; three-ranked, in three rows
Ray (1) Floret on the margin of the flower head of members of the family Compositae when different from those of the centre
(2) Radiating branch of an umbel
Recurved Bent downwards or backwards
Reflexed Bent abruptly or markedly backwards
Rhachis see Rachis
Rhizome Root-like, thickish stem, normally creeping under or half in and half out of the ground, which sends rootlets down and from which branches, stems, leaves and flowering shoots rise upwards

Rosette Dense cluster of leaves resembling in their arrangement the even spacing of petals of a double rose

Rotundate Intermediate between orbicular and oblong

Sagittate Arrow-shaped (see p. 22)

Scabrid Scabrous

Scabrous Rough to the touch, covered with small projections

Scale Specialised leaf or bract, especially the protective covering of a bud, not resembling a leaf but more like a small flat plate-like covering

Scandent Climbing

Scape Leafless flower stalk springing from root

Sclerophyllous Hard-leaved, having much fibre and a thick wall

Scorpioid Having the main stem coiled during development

Scrambler Plant producing long, weak shoots by which it grows over other plants

Sepal Any of the separate parts of the calyx of a flower, one of the outer perianth leaves (usually relatively small and green) (see p. 16)

Septate Divided by one or more partitions

Septum Partition

Serrate Toothed like a saw, with regular pointed teeth pointing upwards and outwards (see p. 22)

Serrulate Minutely serrate

Sessile Without a stalk

Setaceous Bristle-like

Sheath Protective covering

Simple Unbranched or undivided

Sinuate Uneven or wavy, with rather marked or deep undulations

Spatulate Having a narrow base and a broad rounded apex

Spathe Large bract enclosing inflorescence of any of several members of the lily family

Spicate Arranged on a spike

Spike An inflorescence or arrangement of flowers with the flower sessile (without stalks) along an unbranched axis or stem, the lower flowers opening first

Spinose Beset or covered with spikes or thorns

Spur Slender, usually hollow, extension of part of an individual flower, usually containing nectar sought by visiting pollinators (see p. 16)

Stalk Supporting stem

Stamen Male organ of a flower, consisting of pollen sacs (anthers) and usually a stalk (filament) (see p. 16)

Staminal Pertaining to a stamen (e.g. staminal tube, staminal column – the tube, column, formed by stamens united by their filaments)

Staminode A sterile or abortive stamen, or its homologue, without an anther

Standard Large posterial petal of a papilionaceous flower; it is the outside petal in the bud (see p. 16)

Stellate Star-shaped

Stem Main axis of a plant

Stigma Terminal part of the ovary, where pollen enters the gynoecium (see p. 16)

Stipel Stipule at the base of a leaflet, not a leaf

Stipule Leaf-like or scale-like appendage of a leaf, usually at the base of the stalk (petiole)

Stolon Slender horizontal stem that grows along surface of soil and propogates by producing roots and shoots at the nodes or tips; a runner

GLOSSARY

Strigose Covered with appressed bristles

Sub- Nearly, slightly or under, as in many compound words

Subtend Hold or extend underneath, of a bract, stem etc; to have growing in its axil; to enclose or embrace

Style Narrowed upper part of a pistil bearing the stigma

Tendril Twining stalk, not leaf-bearing

Tepal A segment of the perianth where the inner and outer petals look alike

Terete Cylindrical or tapering and round in cross-section

Terminal Borne at the end (of a branch, stalk etc)

Ternate Arranged in whorls or clusters of three

Throat Mouth of the corolla tube

Tomentellous Shortly tomentose

Tomentose Densely covered with short soft hairs

Tooth Short projection on the margin of a leaf, especially if sharp and pointing outwards

Tube Long hollow cylinder, especially used of the lower often long portion of a calyx or corolla

Tumid Swollen

Umbel Inflorescence in which the divergent pedicels or peduncles spring from the same point, as in the spokes of an umbrella

Valvate (1) With margins meeting not overlapping
          (2) Opening into valves

Variety Division of a species

Venation Arrangement of veins on a leaf or leaflet

Verticil Circular arrangement of parts about an axis, especially leaves round a stem

Verticillate Arranged in whorls or verticils

Vibratile Quivering, easily shaken

Villose Shaggy with long weak hairs

Viscid Sticky or glutinous

Whorl Group of three or more similar parts arranged in a circle about an axis, which may be pedicel, peduncle or stalk

Wing (1) Any flat membranous expansion
        (2) One of the two lateral petals of a papilionaceous flower

Zygomorphic Having only one plane along which it can be dissected so that the two halves are mirror images

Suggestions for further reading

AGNEW, A.D.Q. *Upland Wild Flowers of Kenya* (Oxford University Press, 1974)
DALE, I.R. and GREENWAY, P.J. *Kenya Trees and Shrubs* (Buchanan Kenya Estates Limited, 1961)
Flora of Tropical East Africa (Various authors, 1931)
  Published in continuing family parts; 108 parts available. Obtainable at Royal Botanic Gardens, Kew and Text Book Centre, Nairobi.
LIND, E.M. and TALLANTIRE A.C. *Some Common Flowering Plants of Uganda.* (1962)

Picture credits

Colour Index

Plants in which blossoms are streaked, tipped or blotched with secondary colours are listed under their main colour, those in which blossoms may be of several colours or of combined colours are listed under each colour. Page references (in roman type) are to the main text on the species. Plate references (in **bold** type) may be to the species in another colour form since only one example of each species is illustrated. Figures in brackets refer to photographs on plates.

Under each colour heading plants are listed by family in the same sequence as the main text and then by genus and species alphabetically. The cone-bearing Cycads are listed first.

GREYISH-WHITE

Amaranthaceae	*Cyathula cylindrica* 35, **2** (13)
	Pupalia lappacea 36
Malvaceae	*Hibiscus cannabinus* 49, **36** (228)
Loranthaceae	*Loranthus panganensis* 66, **28** (179)
Compositae	*Echinops angustilobus* 80, **3** (20)
	E. hispidus 81
	Tarchonanthus camphoratus 87, **4** (29)
Oranbanchaceae	*Orobanche minor* 101
Gramineae	*Cenchrus ciliaris* 128, **2** (12)

WHITE

Ranunculaceae	*Delphinium leroyi* 26
Nymphaeaceae	*Nymphaea lotus* 27, **8** (48)
Capparaceae	*Gynandropsis gynandra* 29, **3** (17)
	Maerua edulis 29, **11** (70)
Crassulaceae	*Crassula alba* 30, **11** (68)
	C. alsinoides 30
	C. pentandra 30, **33** (213)
Polygonaceae	*Polygonum salicifolium* 33
	P. senegalense 33
Aramanthaceae	*Gomphrena celosiodes* 36, **11** (72)
Geraniaceae	*Geranium aculeatum* 37
	Monsonia ovata 37, **14** (92)
	M. angustifolia 37
	Pelargonium alchemilloides 38
Balsaminaceae	*Impatiens sodenii* 39, **44** (287)
Thymelaeaceae	*Gnidia subcordata* 40, **7** (43)
Proteaceae	*Protea kilimandscharica* 41, **9** (57)
Flacourtiaceae	*Oncoba routledgei* 41, **8** (49)
	O. spinosa 41
Cucurbitaceae	*Peponium vogelii* 43, **14** (90)
Combretaceae	*Combretum aculeatum* 44, **9** (60)
	Terminalia prunioides 44, **10** (62)
Tiliaceae	*Grewia tenax* 46, **5** (34)
Sterculiaceae	*Dombeya rotundifolia* 47, **9** (58)
Malvaceae	*Hibiscus flavifolius* 49, **9** (56)
	H. fuscus 49, **9** (55)
	Pavonia urens 51, **35** (220)
Malpighiaceae	*Caucanthus albidus* 51, **10** (61)
Rosaceae	*Alchemilla fischeri* 53, **15** (30)
	Hagenia abyssinica 53, **30** (194)
Caesalpiniaceae	*Delonix elata* 55, **24** (150)
Papilionaceae	*Trifolium rueppellianum* 62, **39** (249)
	T. semipilosum 63
Mimosaceae	*Acacia mellifera* 65
Umbelliferae	*Caucalis incognita* 69
	Haplosciadium abyssinicum 69, **10** (66)

WHITE contd.

Verbenaceae	*Chascanum hildebrandtii* 108, **2** (10)
	Clerodendrum rotundifolium 108, **3** (15)
	Lippia javanica 109, **8** (54)
	L. ukambensis 109
Labiatae	*Becium sp. A* 110, **1** (6)
	B. obovatum 110, **1** (5)
	Leonotis mollissima 111, **24** (153)
	Leucas grandis 111, **7** (45)
	L. masaiensis 111
	L. urticifolia 111, **3** (19)
	Salvia coccinea var. *lactea* 112, **4** (22)
	S. nilotica 113
Commelinaceae	*Cyanotis barbata* 115, **32** (201)
	C. foecunda 115
Liliaceae	*Chlorophytum blepharophyllum* 117
	C. gallabatense 118
	C. macrophyllum 118
	C. micranthum 118
	C. tenuifolium 117, **3** (14)
	Ornithogallum donaldsonii 119, **3** (21)
	O. gracillimum 119
	O. longibracteatum 119
	Trachyandra saltii 120, **40** (253)
Amaryllidaceae	*Crinum macowanii* 121, **33** (210)
Iridaceae	*Gladiolus ukambanensis* 123, **2** (8)
Orchidaceae	*Bonatea steudneri* 125, **2** (8)
	Diaphananthe fragrantissima 125, **6** (36)
	D. pulchella 125
	Microcoelia smithii 127
	M. guyoniana 126
	Rangaeris amaniensis 126, **4** (23)
	Satyrium crassicaule 127
	S. sacculatum 127

CREAM

Ranunculaceae	*Clematis brachiata* 26, **7** (47)
	C. sinensis 26
Nymphaeaceae	*Nymphaea lotus* 27, **8** (48)
Hydnoraceae	*Hydnora abyssinica* 27, **29** (186)
Phytolaccaceae	*Phytolacca dodecandra* 34, **6** (40)
Aramanthaceae	*Cyathula polycephala* 35, **10** (67)
Zygophyllaceae	*Tribulus cistoides* 36, **19** (123)
Malvaceae	*Hibiscus flavifolius* 49, **9** (56)
	Pavonia zeylonica 51, **14** (91)
Malpighiaceae	*Caucanthus albidus* 51, **10** (61)
Caesalpiniaceae	*Bauhinia taitensis* 54, **12** (76)
	Delonix elata 55, **24** (150)
Mimosaceae	*Acacia drepanolobium* 64, **10** (64)

144

YELLOW contd.
Papilionaceae contd.

YELLOW contd.
Compositae contd.   *S. j.* subsp. *dalei* 86
                     S. j. subsp. *elgonensis* 86
                     S. keniodendron 86
                     Senecio syringifolius 86, **4** (27)
                     Tagetes minuta 87, **18** (118)
                     Taraxacum officinale 87, **17** (103)
Convolvulaceae   *Ipomoea obscura* 98, **13** (87)
                     I. ochracea 98
                     Merremia sp.* 98, **22** (140)
                     M. pinnata 98
                     M. ampelophylla 98
Scrophulariaceae   *Verbascum sinaiticum* 101, **18** (116)
Orobanchaceae   *Cistanche tubulosa* 101, **12** (74)
Acanthaceae   *Barleria eranthemoides* 103, **10** (63)
                     Crossandra stenostachya 105
                     Justicia flava 106, **12** (80)
                     Thunbergia alata 107, **24** (151)
Commelinaceae   *Aneilema acquinoctiale* 114
Liliaceae   *Bulbine abyssinica* 117, **13** (85)
                     Kniphophia thomsonii 119
Iridiceae   *Gladiolus natalensis* 123, **25** (157)
Hypoxidaceae   *Hypoxis obtusa* 124, **21** (133)
                     H. villosa 124
                     H. multiflora 124
Orchidaceae   *Ansellia gigantea* var. *nilotica* 124, **22** (137)
                     Eulophia stenophylla 126, **22** (138)

ORANGE

Nymphaeaceae   *Nymphaea caerulea* 27, **47** (304)
Crassulaceae   *Kalanchoe lanceolata* 31, **25** (155)
Portulacaceae   *Portulaca foliosa* 32
Cactaceae   *Opuntia vulgaris* 43 **24** (152)
Hypericaceae   *Hypericum annulatum* 45, **23** (147)
Malvaceae   *Abutilon hirtum* 48, **23** (146)
Rosaceae   *Hagenia abyssinica* 53, **30** (194)
Papilionaceae   *Rhynchosia usambarensis* 61, **22** (141)
                     Tephrosia holstii 61, **25** (158)
                     Vigna schimperi 63
Compositae   *Crassocephalum vitellinum* 80, **20** (126)
                     Gynura amplexicaulis 82
                     G. miniata 82, **21** (132)
                     G. scandens 83
                     G. valeriana 83
                     Senecio syringifolius 86, **4** (27)
                     Spilanthes mauritiana 87, **15** (97)
                     Tithonia diversifolia 88, **17** (109)
Campanulaceae   *Canarina abyssinica* 90, **27** (168, 169)
                     C. eminii 90

146

COLOUR INDEX

147

COLOUR INDEX

PINK contd.

Orchidaceae *Disa hircicornis* 125
D. scutellifera 126
D. stairsii 126
Satyrium cheirophorum 127
S. crassicaule 127

MAGENTA

Capparaceae	*Cleome allamannii* 28, **43** (276)
Aizoaceae	*Delosperma oehleri* 32, **36** (231)
Portulaceae	*Talinum portulacifolium* 32, **43** (275)
Aramanthaceae	*Centemopsis kirkii* 35, **43** (278)
Geraniaceae	*Geranium ocellatum* 37, **41** (266)
Oxalidaceae	*Oxalis latifolia* 38
Nyctaginaceae	*Commicarpus pedunculosus* 40, **39** (248)
Tiliaceae	*Grewia lilacina* 46, **34** (217)
	G. similis 46, **34** (216)
Papilionaceae	*Vigna* sp. * 63, **38** (242)
Rutaceae	*Calodendrum capense* 68, **34** (214)
Asclepiadaceae	*Gomphocarpus semilunatus* 73
Rubiaceae	*Pentas zanzibarica* 76
Campanulaceae	*Lobelia holstii* 91, **39** (251)
Boraginaceae	*Echiochilon lithospermoides* 93, **45** (292)
Scrophulariaceae	*Craterostigma pumilum* 99
	Pseudosopubia hildebrandtii 100, **32** (206)
Acanthaceae	*Acanthus pubescens* 103
	Justicia declipteroides 106, **41** (263)
Labiatae	*Satureia pseudosimensis* 113, **36** (229)
Orchidaceae	*Disa stairsii* 126

PURPLE

Portulacaceae	*Talinum portulacifolium* 32, **43** (277)
Aramanthaceae	*Digera muricata* 35, **37** (234)
Oxalidaceae	*Oxalis obliquifolia* 38, **34** (218)
Balsaminaceae	*Impatiens pseudoviola* 39
Nyctaginaceae	*Commicarpus pedunculosus* 40, **39** (248)
Malvaceae	*Hibiscus cannabinus* 49, **36** (228)
Rosaceae	*Rubus steudneri* 53, **33** (212)
Papilionaceae	*Rhynchosia albissima* 61
	Tephrosia interrupta 62, **31** (196)
	Trifolium burchellianum subsp. *johnstonii* 62, **42** (272)
	T. rueppellianum 62, **39** (249)
	Vigna sp. * 63, **38** (242)
Umbelliferae	*Caucalis incognita* 69
Asclepiadaceae	*Calotropis procera* 71, **42** (273)
	Caralluma foetida 72, **30** (193)
	C. speciosa 72
	C. socotrana 72
	Gomphocarpus fruticosus 73
	Edithcolea grandis 73, **23** (144)

COLOUR INDEX

PURPLE contd.

Compositae
Bothriocline fusca 79
Carduus chamaecephalus 79
C. millefolius 79
Cirsium vulgare 79, **37** (237)
Ethulia sp. A. 81, **36** (230), **2** (11)
E. scheffleri 81, **31** (195)
Gutenbergia cordifolia 82, **38** (244)
G. fischeri 82, **39** (250)
G. rueppellii 82
Hoehnelia vernonioides 84, **37** (236)
Lactuca glandulifera 84
Senecio roseiflorus 86, **39** (247)
Sphaeranthus napierae 86, **36** (226)
S. suaveolens 87, **37** (233)
Vernonia auriculifera 88, **44** (283)
V. aemulans 88

Campanulaceae
Lobelia holstii 91, **39** (251)
L. keniensis 91, **48** (308)
L. telekii 91, **48** (311)
Wahlenbergia abyssinica 91, **46** (296)

Solanaceae
Solanum sp. * 95, **44** (282)
S. aculeatissimum 95
S. sessilistellatum 94, **43** (277)

Convolvulaceae
Ipomoea cicatricosa 96, **37** (238)
I. hildebrandtii 97, **40** (259)
I. mombassana 97, **40** (257)

Orobanchaceae
Orobanche minor 101

Acanthaceae
Dyschoriste sp. * 105, **32** (203)
Justicia sp. * 106, **38** (246)
J. diclipteroides 106, **41** (263)
Thunbergia holstii 107, **45** (289)

Verbenaceae
Verbena bonariensis 109, **37** (239)

Labiatae
Erythrochlamys spectabilis 110, **39** (252)
Nepeta azurea 112, **42** (270)
Salvia merjamie 113, **45** (293)
S. nilotica 113
Satureia pseudosimensis 113, **36** (229)

Liliaceae
Scilla kirkii 120, **42** (269)
S. indica 120

Indaceae
Dierama pendulum 122

Orchidaceae
Diaphananthe rutila 125
Eulophia horsfallii 126, **38** (245)

MAUVE

Capparaceae
Cleome allamanui 28, **43** (276)
Gynandropsis gynandra 29, **3** (17)

Geraniaceae
Geranium aculeatum 37
Monsonia angustifolia 37

Balsaminaceae
Impatiens meruensis subsp. cruciata 39

151

MAUVE contd.

Tiliaceae	*Grewia lilacina* 46, **34** (217)
	G. similis 46, **34** (216)
Malvaceae	*Abutilon longicuspe* 48, **42** (267)
	Pavonia urens 51, **35** (220)
Papilionaceae	*Millettia dura* 60
	Trifolium cryptopodium 62, **43** (279)
	Vigna vexillata 63, **38** (243)
	V. monophylla 63
Mimosaceae	*Dichrostachys cinerea* subsp. *cinerea* 65, **31** (198)
Asclepiadaceae	*Calotropis procera* 71, **42** (273)
Rubiaceae	*Pentas lanceolata* 75, **41** (262)
Compositae	*Bothriocline tomentosa* 79, **34** (219)
	Sphaeranthus gomphrenoides 87
	Vernonia auriculifera 88, **44** (283)
	V. galamensis 88
	V. afromontana 88
Campanulaceae	*Lobelia holstii* 91, **39** (251)
Solanaceae	*Solanum* sp. * 95, **44** (282)
	S. incanum 94, **44** (284)
	S. taitense 95
Convolvulaceae	*Ipomoea cairica* 96, **40** (258)
Scrophulariaceae	*Craterostigma plantagineum* 99, **45** (290)
	Ghikaea speciosa 100, **38** (241)
	Veronica abyssinica 101, **47** (304)
Acanthaceae	*Dyschoriste* sp. * 105, **32** (203)
	Hypoestes aristata 106
	H. verticillaris 105, **41** (260)
	Justicia sp. * 106, **38** (246)
	Thunbergia battiscombei 107
Verbenaceae	*Lantana camara* 109, **31** (197)
Labiatae	*Plectranthus caninus* 112
Commelinaceae	*Cyanotis barbata* 115, **32** (201)
	Murdannia clarkeana 115
	M. semiteres 115
	M. simplex 115, **43** (274)
Iridaceae	*Romulea fischeri* 123, **38** (240)
	R. keniensis 123
Orchidaceae	*Eulophia horsfallii* 126, **38** (245)
	Satyrium crassicaule 127

BLUE

Ranunculaceae	*Delphinium macrocentron* 26, **48** (310)
	D. wellbyi 2
Nymphaeaceae	*Nymphaea caerulea* 27, **47** (305)
Papilionaceae	*Clitoria ternatea* 56, **46** (299)
Rubiaceae	*Pentanisia ouranogyne* 75, **45** (288)
Compositae	*Felicia abyssinica* subsp. *neghellensis* 82
	F. muricata 81, **48** (309)
	Lactuca capensis 84

BLUE contd.

Plumbaginaceae	*Ceratostigma abyssinicum* 90, **47** (302)
Campanulaceae	*Lobelia keniensis* 91, **48** (308)
Boraginaceae	*Cynoglossum amplifolium* 93
	C. coeruleum 93
	C. geometricum 92
	C. lancifolium 92, **46** (294)
Solanaceae	*Solanum* sp. * 95, **44** (282)
	S. incanum 94, **44** (284)
	S. nakurense 95
Scrophulariaceae	*Craterostigma plantagineum* 99, **45** (290)
	C. pumilum 99
	Veronica abyssinica 101, **47** (304)
Acanthaceae	*Acanthus eminens* 103, **47** (303)
	Barleria acanthoides 103, **1** (1)
	B. spinisepala 104, **46** (295)
	B. submollis 104, **40** (256)
	Blepharis linariifolia 104, **46** (298)
	Brillantaisia nitens 104, **41** (264)
	Ecbolium hamatum 105
	E. revolutum 105, **47** (307)
Verbenaceae	*Clerodendrum myricoides* 108, **44** (285)
Labiatae	*Plectranthrus barbatus* 112, **47** (301)
	P. caninus 112
	P. cylindraceus 112, **42** (268)
	P. sylvestris 112, **44** (281)
Commelinaceae	*Aneilema hockii* 114
	Anthericopsis sepalosa 114, **40** (255)
	Commelina sp. A 114, **47** (307)
	C. benghalensis 114
	C. forskalei 114, **46** (300)
	C. latifolia 114
	Cyanotis barbata 115, **32** (201)
	Murdannia clarkeana 115
	M. semiteres 115, **43** (274)
Liliaceae	*Scilla indica* 120
	S. kirkii 120, **42** (269)
Iridaceae	*Aristea alata* 122
	A. angolensis 122

BROWN

Polygonaceae	*Rumex bequaertii* 34
	R. ruwenzoriensis 34
Papilionaceae	*Eriosema jurionum* 58
	Vigna schimperi 63
Asclepiadaceae	*Gomphocarpus kaessneri* 73, **15** (99)
	Stapelia semota 74, **22** (139)
Rubiaceae	*Galium aparinoides* 74
Compositae	*Helichrysum cymosum* subsp. *fruticosum* 83, **16** (102)
Iridaceae	*Gladiolus natalensis* 123, **25** (157)
Orchidaceae	*Satyrium sacculatum* 127

Alphabetical Index

Family names and common names are in ordinary type; scientific generic and specific names are in *italics*. References to text pages are in ordinary type and to plates in **bold** type (with individual photographs in brackets). Synonyms are listed with a reference to the name under which they are described.

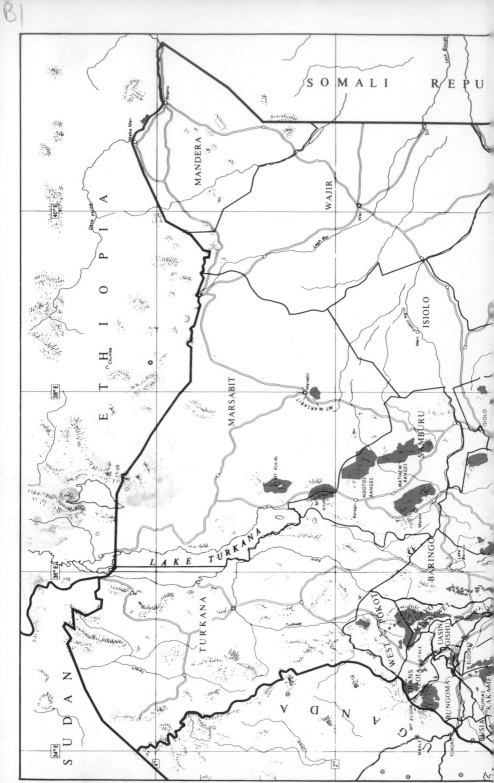